P9-BZD-305

GREAT AMERICAN QUILTS 2003

Edited by
Rhonda Richards

Oxmoor House

Great American Quilts 2003

©2002 by Oxmoor House, Inc.
Book Division of Southern Progress Corporation
P.O. Box 2463, Birmingham, Alabama 35201

Published by Oxmoor House, Inc., and Leisure Arts, Inc.

All rights reserved. No part of this book may be reproduced in any form or by any means without the prior written permission of the publisher, excepting brief quotes in connection with reviews written specifically for inclusion in magazines or newspapers, or single copies for strictly personal use.

Library of Congress Catalog Number: 2002106188
Hardcover ISBN: 0-8487-2561-1
Softcover ISBN: 0-8487-2562-X
Printed in the United States of America
First Printing 2002
To order additional publications, call 800-633-4910.

For more books to enrich your life, visit:
oxmoorhouse.com

Editor-in-Chief: Nancy Fitzpatrick Wyatt
Executive Editor: Katherine M. Eakin
Art Director: Cynthia R. Cooper

Editor: Rhonda Richards
Contributing Copy Editor and Technical Writer:
    Laura Morris Edwards
Editorial Assistant: Andrea Carver
Designer/Illustrator: Kelly Davis
Senior Photographer: Jim Bathie
Senior Photo Stylist: Kay Clarke
Photographer: Brit Huckabay
Photo Stylist: Ashley Wyatt
Contributing Photographer: Keith Harrelson
Contributing Photo Stylist: Cathy Harris
Publishing Systems Administrator: Rick Tucker
Director, Production and Distribution: Phillip Lee
Book Production Manager: Theresa L. Beste
Production Assistant: Faye Porter Bonner

Cover: *Sunday Quilt,* page 88

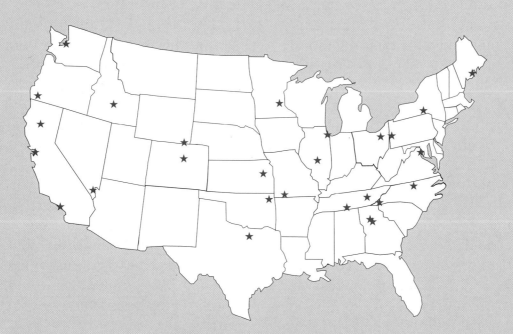

Where do Great American Quilts come from? They come from the north, south, east, and west, and lots of places in between. This year's book features quilters from 21 states. If your state is not represented, perhaps you can make a mark on next year's map. (We'd love to hear from states not represented in our history—Delaware, South Dakota, and Montana—as well as Washington, D.C., and the territories.) To submit a quilt for consideration, send a snapshot with your name, address, and phone number to *Great American Quilts* Submissions, Oxmoor House, 2100 Lakeshore Drive, Birmingham, AL 35209. Deadline for the 2004 edition is January 10, 2003. Sorry, we cannot return photos.

From The Editor

God Bless America

"Terrorist attacks can shake the foundations of our biggest buildings, but they cannot touch the foundation of America. These acts shatter steel, but they cannot dent the steel of American resolve."

—*President George W. Bush, September 11, 2001*

The September attacks occurred only weeks before we began gathering quilts for *Great American Quilts 2003*. Americans drew close to one another physically and emotionally, ready to help wherever possible. Quilters were quick to respond, sending quilts to victims' families, or making quilts for their own local Red Cross and other emergency services. Then, in November, there was the *America: From the Heart* exhibit at the International Quilt Festival in Houston, Texas, that reminded us what it meant to be an American. We were reminded how we can use our talents to bring comfort to others. Even if we couldn't wrap our arms around someone and say, "I care," our quilts could.

Patriotism still swells in our country, so we thought it appropriate to share quilts of **American Spirit** in this edition. From traditional red-and-white *Feathered Star* quilts to the flag-waving *God Bless America,* you're sure to find a project to express your love for our country.

Quilts Across America features quilts from New York to California. We have two interpretations of the Oak Leaf: the traditional *Oak Leaves & Anvil* and the funky *Autumn Oaks Plaid.* If you like graphic impact, try *Kinetic Energy* or the prize-winning *Frightened by a Bag of M&Ms.*

Traditions in Quilting features American classics stitched in both reproduction and contemporary fabrics. If you're an Aunt Grace fabric collector, you'll enjoy seeing the *Scrapbag Schoolhouse* quilt that launched Judie Rothermel's career as a fabric designer.

Bee Quilters are back! This chapter showcases our cover project, *Sunday Quilt,* along with other spectacular group projects such as *Hidden Circles* and *Springtime Dogwoods in the Ozarks.* Uncover a great way to use friendship blocks in *Words of Wisdom,* and discover a homespun classic from our friends at Little Quilts.

As always, our **Designer Gallery** features art quilts made by award-winning and nationally known quilt artists. Although these one-of-a-kind quilts cannot be duplicated, let them inspire you to make your own masterpiece.

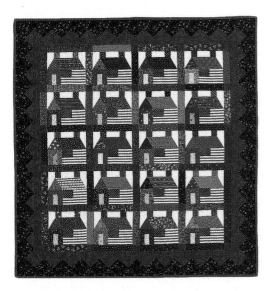

American Spirit

Quilts Across America

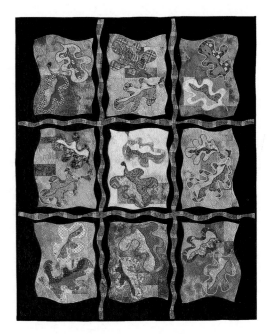

Traditions in Quilting

Bee Quilters

Designer Gallery

American Spirit

Pat Sloan
Herndon, Virginia

When Pat Sloan first began quilting in 1978, she never dreamed it would become a full-time business for her. She made her first quilt because she needed a bedspread. "I bought a magazine, made the top, used a sheet for the back, and tied the quilt every four feet or so," says Pat. It seemed like enough at the time!" A few years later, her friend Gwyn insisted that she sign up for a quilting class. "I was hooked by the end of the evening, and I have not stopped since," recalls Pat.

For the last 10 years, Pat has been an active member of the Reston Chapter of Quilters Unlimited in northern Virginia, serving as program chairperson, hospitality coordinator, and president. She also stitches with a dear group of friends who call themselves the Folk Art Group. "Not all of us quilt," says Pat. "Many just stitch, and we also enjoy other old-time crafts such as penny rugs and rug hooking. These ladies are my true kindred spirits."

"I've found that quilting has fueled my spirit, both in a creative sense and for my total well being."

Although Pat has always been "a maker of things," she believes she found her true calling when she discovered quilting. "I've found that quilting has fueled my spirit, both in a creative sense and for my total well being," says Pat. "I love color, I love design, and I love the feel of cloth. The world of quilt art is never ending. I can, and have, expanded into different styles as my skills and interests have changed."

Pat began designing her own quilt patterns in 1998 and turned it into a full-time business in 2000. To see more of her work, visit her Web site at www.quiltershome.com.

American Pie
2001

Pat Sloan is drawn to old quilts and likes to include features typical of their style in her own quilts.

"I adore stars and swags, so that became my border idea," says Pat. "The red, cream, and blue color scheme came about because I wanted an Americana look with an old quilt feel."

The blocks are oak leaf variations, often seen in fine antique quilts. Most traditional appliqué quilts use one fabric, often a solid, for the background. In Pat's quilt, she used a variety of pieces—in this case, an assortment of fat eighths (9" x 22" pieces). The dots add a touch of whimsy.

"I love piecing the background, because it gives the quilt much more interest and movement than just using one piece of background fabric," says Pat.

Note that Pat also used a variety of fabrics in the reds and blues, which keeps the eye moving across the quilt.

American Pie

Finished Size
Quilt: 64½" x 64½"
Blocks: 9 (15½" x 15½")

Materials
18 (9" x 22") fat eighths light
  prints for blocks
9 assorted ½ yard cuts navy
  prints for appliqué, sashing,
  and outer border
3 assorted ½ yard cuts red prints
  for appliqué
1½ yards red print for inner
  border, sashing squares, and
  binding
½ yard gold-with-stars for
  appliqué
4 yards backing fabric
Twin-size batting
Freezer paper for templates

Making Patterns
Due to their large size, we had to halve and quarter two patterns. Follow the instructions below to make freezer-paper templates. Patterns are on pages 12–13.
1. Cut 1 (16") square from freezer paper. Fold it in half horizontally and vertically to divide the piece into 4 equal quadrants. Open paper and align corner of ¼ Oak Spray with center of 1 quadrant. Trace pattern on paper side.
2. Fold paper back into quadrants along fold lines. Cut along drawn lines and open to reveal full pattern.
3. Cut 1 (7" x 20") rectangle from freezer paper. Fold in half crosswise to make a center crease. Open paper and align it over Swag pattern on page 13 so that the dashed line falls at the

crease. Trace half pattern on paper side.
4. Fold rectangle in half again along crease. Cut along drawn lines and open to reveal full pattern.

Cutting
Instructions are for rotary cutting and quick piecing. Border strips are exact length needed. You may want to cut them longer to allow for piecing variations. Patterns are on pages 12–13. **Cut pieces in order listed to make best use of yardage.**
From each fat eighth of light prints, cut:
• 2 (8¼") squares for blocks.
From each navy print, cut:
• 1 (2½" x 42") strip. Cut strip into 1 or 2 (2½" x 16") sashing

strips. You will need 12 total, and you may piece strips for variety.
• 1 (14") square. Cut 1 oak spray from square.
• 2 (6½" x 28") strips. Cut strips into 4 (6½" x 12½") segments for outer border.
From each red print, cut:
• 3 sets of 4 block arcs.
• 4 border swags.
From red border print, cut:
• 4 (1½" x 54") lengthwise strips. Cut strips into 2 (1½" x 51") inner side borders and 2 (1½" x 53") inner top and bottom borders.
• 5 (2¼" x 54") lengthwise strips for binding.
• 4 (2½") sashing squares.
From gold-with-stars, cut:
• 36 circles for blocks.
• 12 stars for outer border.

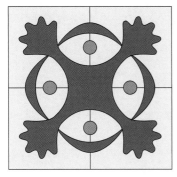

Block Assembly Diagram

Block Assembly

Refer to *Block Assembly Diagram* throughout.

1. Lay out 4 assorted 8¼" squares. Join to make block background. Appliqué 1 oak spray, 4 matching red arcs, and 4 gold circles as shown to complete 1 block. Blanket-stitch in matching thread, if desired.

2. Make 9 appliquéd blocks.

Blanket Stitch Diagram

Quilt Assembly

Refer to *Quilt Top Assembly Diagram* and photo throughout.

1. Lay out blocks, sashing strips, and sashing squares. Join into rows; join rows to complete center.

2. Add inner red side borders to quilt. Add inner top and bottom borders.

3. Join assorted navy segments to make 2 (6½" x 53") outer top and bottom borders. Add to quilt.

4. Join assorted navy segments to make 2 (6½" x 65") outer side borders. Add to quilt.

5. Appliqué on borders: 3 swags and 2 stars on each side, centering stars on sashing strips. Appliqué 1 star in each corner. Blanket-stitch edges in matching thread, if desired.

Quilting and Finishing

1. Divide backing fabric into 2 (2-yard) lengths. Cut 1 piece in half lengthwise. Sew 1 narrow panel to each side of wide panel. Press seam allowances toward narrow panels.

2. Layer backing, batting, and quilt top; baste. Quilt as desired. Quilt shown is meander-quilted in matching thread.

3. Join 2¼"-wide red strips into 1 continuous piece for straight-grain French-fold binding. Add binding to quilt.

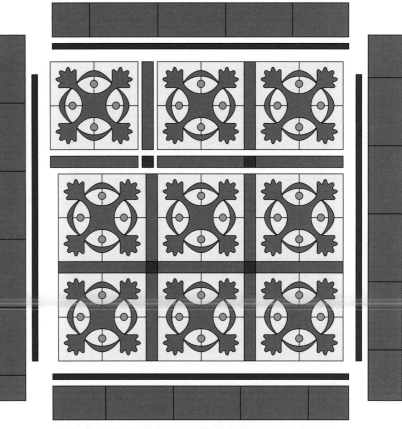

Quilt Top Assembly Diagram

Trace, scan, or photocopy this quilt label to finish your quilt.

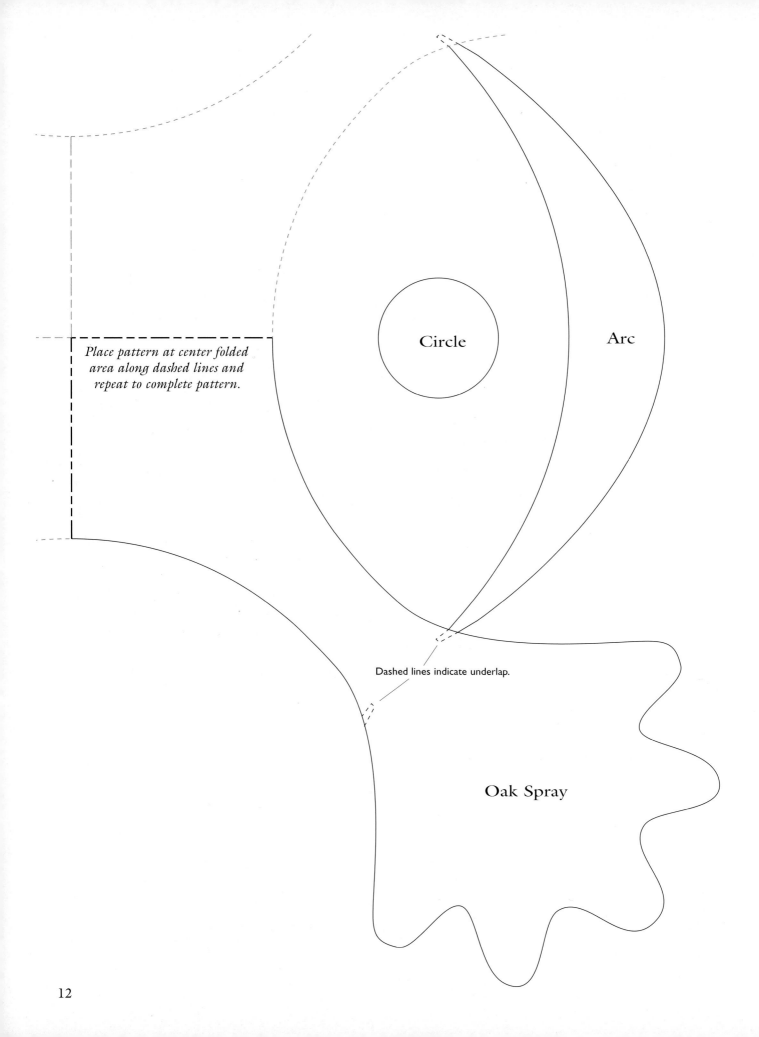

Place pattern at center folded area along dashed lines and repeat to complete pattern.

Circle

Arc

Dashed lines indicate underlap.

Oak Spray

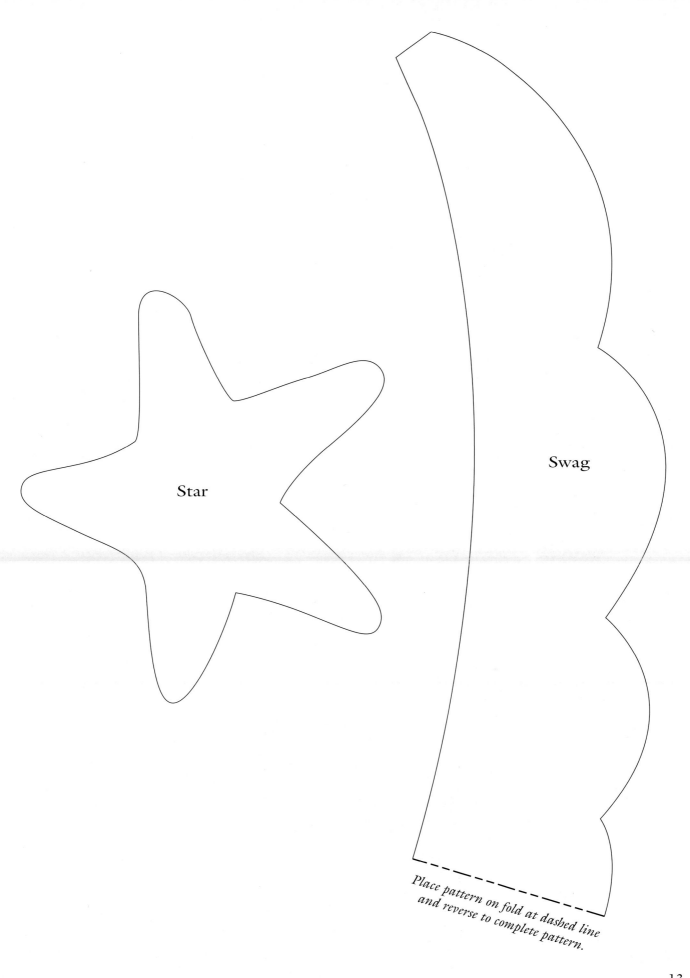

Star

Swag

Place pattern on fold at dashed line and reverse to complete pattern.

13

Carolyn Sundberg
Alpharetta, GA

*L*ike many quilters, Carolyn Sundberg started sewing garments when she was in high school. She made her first quilt in 1973 by cutting up old shirts, skirts, and aprons. "It's not a very pretty quilt," says Carolyn, "but it has a lot of sentimental value, and I use it as a tree skirt at Christmas."

Carolyn believes that her great respect for traditional blocks and patterns comes from her New England upbringing. She welcomes the challenge of taking a few simple blocks and combining them with sashing and borders to make a new and exciting quilt.

"For the past four years, I've gone to the American Quilter's Society show in Paducah, Kentucky, with friends from my guild," says Carolyn. "I always come home with a car full of fabric, a notebook full of ideas, and renewed enthusiasm for my favorite hobby. I've made many wonderful quilting friends over the years, and it's always a joy to share my love of quilting with them. Quilting is a passion to me, from the initial inspiration to the final stitch in the label. It's truly an exciting and rewarding experience."

"... I always come home with a car full of fabric, a notebook full of ideas, and renewed enthusiasm for my favorite hobby."

Carolyn belongs to the Bulloch Hall Quilt Guild in Roswell, Georgia, where she served as president from 1999–2000, and to the East Cobb Quilter's Guild in Marietta, Georgia. She also belongs to a bee group, the Alphabees.

Liberty Houses
2000

Carolyn has been collecting patriotic fabrics for years. When she saw *An American Household* in Fons and Porter's *For the Love of Quilting* magazine, she knew she had a use for all her beautiful, starry fabric.

The original quilt was designed and made by Carol Olson of Auberry, California. Carolyn tweaked the houses to fit a pre-printed flag fabric she had and changed the borders to a pieced design.

"While hand-quilting it," says Carolyn, "we had a two-day power outage due to an ice storm. So I just snuggled up underneath it, quilting by Coleman lantern. Now I have a new understanding of how difficult it was to quilt without the modern convenience of electric lighting."

Liberty Houses appeared in Bulloch Hall's Great American Cover-Up Quilt Show in March 2000, in Roswell, Georgia. It also won second place in a theme category at the East Cobb Quilter's Guild 8th Biennial Show in Marietta, Georgia, in September 2001.

Liberty Houses

Finished Size
Quilt: 51½" x 56"
Blocks: 20 (8" x 7")

Materials
¾ yard white-on-cream for block background

20 (2" x 3") pieces assorted cream prints for doors

20 (4" x 22") strips assorted red and blue prints for house blocks

20 flags or flag print, each 3¾" x 5½"

5 fat eighths (9" x 22") assorted blue prints for sashing

1½ yards red print for sashing squares, inner border, pieced border, and binding

1 yard blue print for pieced border and outer border

3 yards backing fabric

Twin-size batting

Cutting
Instructions are for rotary cutting and quick piecing. Border strips are exact length needed. You may want to cut them longer to allow for piecing variations. Patterns are on page 17. **Cut pieces in order listed to make best use of yardage.**

From white-on-cream, cut:
- 4 (1¾" x 40") strips. Cut strips into 20 (1¾" x 3") B rectangles, and 40 (1¾" x 2") C rectangles for block background.
- 20 Ds.
- 20 Ds reversed.

From assorted cream prints, cut:
- 20 (1½" x 2¾") I rectangles for doors.

From assorted prints, cut:
- 10 sets red and 10 sets blue of
  - 2 (1¾" x 1¾") As for chimneys.
  - 1 E for roof.
  - 1 F for gable.
  - 1 (1½" x 1½") H and 2 (1½" x 3¾") Js for house front.

From flags or flag print, cut:
- 20 (3¾" x 5½") flags.

From assorted blue prints, cut (across short end):
- 24 (2" x 8½") horizontal sashing strips.
- 25 (2" x 7½") vertical sashing strips.

From red print, cut:
- 2 (2" x 42") strips. Cut strips into 30 (2") sashing squares.
- 5 (2½" x 42") strips. Cut and piece as needed to make 2 (2½" x 40") top and bottom borders and 2 (2½" x 48½") side borders.
- 4 (2⅞" x 42") strips. Cut strips into 48 (2⅞") squares. Cut squares in half diagonally to make 96 border triangles.
- 6 (2¼"-wide) strips for binding.

From blue print, cut:
- 4 (2⅞" x 42") strips. Cut strips into 48 (2⅞") squares. Cut squares in half diagonally to make 96 border triangles.
- 6 (2½" x 42") strips. Cut 2 strips in half. Join 1 strip with 1 half-strip to make 1 outer border. Make 4 outer borders.

Block Assembly
Refer to *Block Assembly Diagram* throughout.

1. Choose 1 set As for chimneys, 1 roof E, 1 gable F, 2 Js and matching 1 H for house front, and 1 I door. Choose 1 flag. Choose 1 B, 2 Cs, 1 D, and 1 D reversed

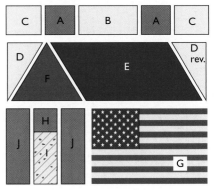

Block Assembly Diagram

from matching background pieces.

2. Work in rows. Lay out 2 As, 1 B, and 2 Cs as shown; join to make top row.

3. Lay out D, F, E, and D rev. as shown. Join to make roof row.

4. Lay out 2 Js , 1 H, and 1 I as shown. Join. Add flag G to make bottom row.

5. Join rows to complete 1 house block. Make 20 House blocks. Vary red and blue sets as desired.

Quilt Assembly
1. Lay out blocks, sashing, and sashing squares as shown in *Quilt Top Assembly Diagram*. Join into rows; join rows to complete quilt center.

2. Add red top and bottom borders to quilt. Add red side borders to quilt.

3. Join 1 each red and blue border triangles to make 1 border unit. Make 96 border units.

Border Unit Diagram

4. Join 22 border units to make top border. Adjust seams as needed for fit. Add to quilt. Repeat for bottom border.

5. Join 26 border units to make 1 side border. Adjust seams as needed for fit. Add to quilt. Repeat for second side border.

6. Center blue outer borders on each side of quilt and add. Miter corners.

Quilting and Finishing

1. Divide backing fabric into 2 (1½-yard) lengths. Cut 1 panel in half lengthwise. Sew 1 narrow panel to 1 side of wide panel. Press seam allowance toward narrow panel. Seam will run horizontally. Remaining panel is extra and may be used to make a hanging sleeve.

2. Layer backing, batting, and quilt top; baste. Quilt as desired. Quilt shown has a zigzag pattern in outer border and six-pointed stars in red border. Houses are echo-quilted in fronts, gables, and flags. Block background is quilted in-the-ditch with stars and moons added.

3. Join 2¼"-wide red print strips into 1 continuous piece for straight-grain French-fold binding. Add binding to quilt.

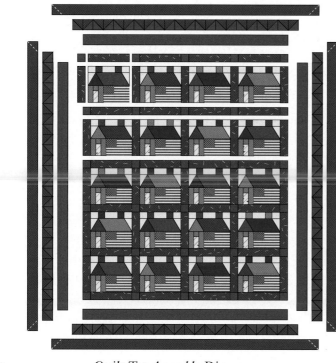

Quilt Top Assembly Diagram

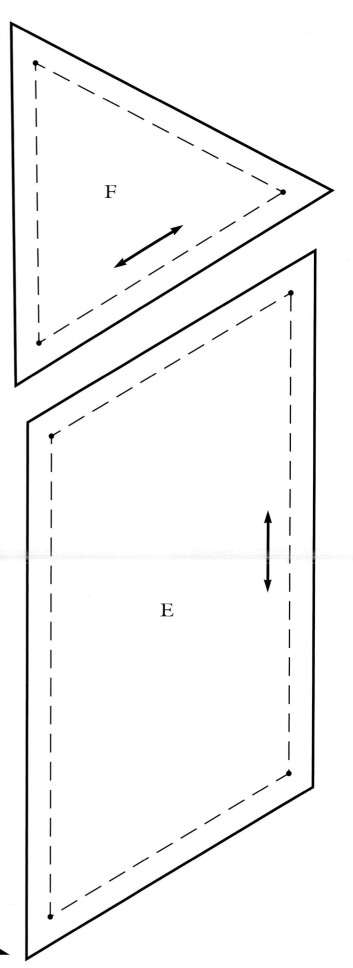

Linda McCuean
New Galilee, Pennsylvania

*A*lthough Linda McCuean has been hand-quilting for more than 24 years, she has only been machine-quilting for four years. One would never guess that, looking at her machine masterpieces!

"I learned to sew as a child, when my mom shipped me off to a 4-H Club," says Linda. "I sewed most of my

"My favorite kind of day is one when I can spend a few hours quilting."

own clothes as a teen and then later for my family and home when our four kids were young." Linda tried her hand at quilting when a Log Cabin pattern caught her attention in a magazine. Although she has taken a few classes through the years, she is mostly self-taught.

"Quilting is a major part of my life," Linda confesses. "My favorite kind of day is one when I can spend a few hours piecing or quilting." Linda works part-time at Amy Baughman's Quilting Department in New Brighton, Pennsylvania. She is also a member of the Beaver Valley Piecemakers guild, and My Quilt Group—a small group of neighborhood friends.

Feathered Star
2000

Linda had been quilting on the Gamill longarm quilting machine for only a year when she made the *Feathered Star*. She designed it as her entry for the 2000 Machine Quilter's Showcase.

"I have enjoyed entering my hand-quilted pieces in shows for some time, so I wanted to create a real heirloom machine quilt," says Linda. "I wanted it to be visually captivating, with lots of contrast and lots of open spaces for elaborate quilting."

Since Feathered Stars are among Linda's favorite blocks, she made nine large stars. When the blocks were done, she laid them out on the living room floor to plan the rest of the quilt.

"I considered a pieced border, but my time was limited," Linda says. "So I decided to set the blocks on point inside a split solid border."

Linda has collected quilting patterns for many years. She marked designs on the top with a blue water-soluble marker. Next she pinned the top and a heavy 20-ounce polyester batt into the machine. She used water-soluble thread to baste the designs for the trapunto (stuffed) areas. Once this was done, she removed the piece from the machine and spent many hours tediously trimming away the batting, leaving only the areas that would stuff the quilting designs. Then she pinned the quilt back into the machine with a thin cotton batt and the backing fabric to start the actual quilting process.

Every seam is stitched in-the-ditch with the white background filled with stipple quilting—small squiggles that don't ovelap. The quilting took Linda 33 hours.

Once the quilting and binding were completed, Linda rinsed the quilt to remove the blue markings and the basting thread, and then blocked the quilt to dry.

Feathered Star

Finished Size

Quilt: 91" x 91"

Blocks: 9 (18½" x 18½")

Materials

4 yards red print

10 yards white

8¼ yards backing fabric

Queen-size batting

Cutting

Instructions are for rotary cutting and quick piecing. Border strips are exact length needed. You may want to make them longer to allow for piecing variations. Patterns are on page 23. **Cut pieces in order listed to make best use of yardage.**

From red print, cut:

- 11 (1⅞" x 42") strips. Cut strips into 216 (1⅞") squares for A units.
- 3 (1½" x 42") strips. Cut strips into 72 (1½") B squares.
- 72 Cs.
- 3 (2½" x 42") strips. Cut strips into 36 (2½") squares for E units.
- 72 Fs.
- 16 (1" x 42") strips for border strip sets.
- 1 (35") square for binding. Make 400" of 2¼"-wide bias.

From white, cut:

- 2¾ yards. Cut yardage into 4 (6½" x 99") lengthwise outer border strips and 4 (2½" x 65") inner border strips.
- 2 (34¾") squares. Cut squares in half diagonally to make 4 large setting triangles.
- 14 (1⅞" x 42") strips. Cut strips into 288 (1⅞") squares for A units.

- 72 Ds.
- 3 (2½" x 42") strips. Cut strips into 36 (2½") squares for E units.
- 3 (9" x 42") strips. Cut strips into 9 (9") squares. Cut squares in quarters diagonally to make 36 G triangles.
- 6 (6" x 42") strips. Cut strips into 36 (6") H squares.
- 8 (1" x 42") strips for border strip sets.

A Unit Assembly Diagram

Block Assembly

1. Referring to *A Unit Assembly*

Diagram, draw a diagonal line from corner to corner on back of white 1⅞" squares. Place 1 red and 1 white square together, right sides facing. Stitch ¼" from line on both sides. Cut apart along drawn line and press open to make 2 A units. Make 432 A units (48 per block).

2. Cut remaining white 1⅞" squares in half diagonally to make 144 white A triangles (16 per block).

3. Cut 2 (2½") red squares in half diagonally to make 4 red E triangles.

4. Referring to *Corner Strip Assembly Diagram*, join 3 A units. Repeat. Join 1 white A triangle and 1 C to each strip. Add 1 B square to 1 strip. Join strips to

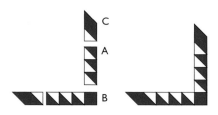

Corner Strip Assembly Diagram

complete 1 corner strip set. Make 4 corner strip sets.

Side Unit Assembly Diagram

5. Referring to *Side Unit Assembly Diagram*, join 3 A units. Repeat. Join 1 white A triangle to each strip. Add 1 B square to 1 strip. Join strips as shown. Add 1 D to 1 side of strip unit. Join 1 red E triangle to 1 D. Join to remaining side to complete 1 side unit. Make 4 side units.

Center Assembly Diagram

6. Referring to *Center Assembly Diagram*, join 8 Fs in pairs to make 4 quadrants. Join quadrants to make center star.

7. Using method in Step 1, make 4 E units from red and white squares. Cut 2 white squares in half diagonally to make 4 E triangles.

8. Set in white E triangles to star. Set in E units in corners to complete block center.

9. Lay out corner strips, side

Block Assembly Diagram 1

Block Assembly Diagram 2

units, and center star as shown in *Block Assembly Diagram 1*. Join into rows; join rows for feathered star.

10. Referring to *Block Assembly Diagram 2*, set in G triangles. Set in H squares to complete 1 Feathered Star block *(Block Diagram)*. Trim block evenly to 19" x 19".

11. Make 9 Feathered Star blocks.

Block Diagram

Quilt Top Assembly Diagram

Quilt Assembly

Refer to *Quilt Top Assembly Diagram* throughout.

1. Lay out blocks in 3 rows of 3 blocks each. Join into rows; join rows.

2. Center 1 white 2½"-wide border on each side and join. Miter corners.

3. Join 2 red and 1 white 1"-wide strips to make 1 border strip set. Make 8 border strip sets.

4. Referring to *Mitered Corner Diagram*, center 1 border strip set on each right angle side of large setting triangles and join. Miter outer corner. Trim opposite raw edge even with triangle edge. Repeat for 4 setting triangles.

5. Center 1 setting triangle on

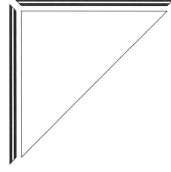

Mitered Corner Diagram

each side of quilt and join. Trim excess white border even with outer edge of border strip sets.

6. Center 1 white 6½"-wide border on each side of quilt and join. Miter corners.

Quilting and Finishing

1. Divide backing fabric into 3 (2¾-yard) lengths. Cut 1 piece in half lengthwise. Sew 1 narrow panel between wide panels. Press seam allowances toward narrow panel. Remaining panel is extra. Seams will run horizontally.

2. Layer backing, batting, and quilt top; baste. Quilt as desired. Quilt shown is heavily quilted with florals, urns, pineapples, and leaves. Background is stippled.

3. Mark scallops on quilt border. There are 13 per side, with half circles on corners, and are on approximately 5⅜" centers, with 4¼" radius. Sew bias binding to front of quilt. Trim scallops. Stitch binding to back of quilt.

22

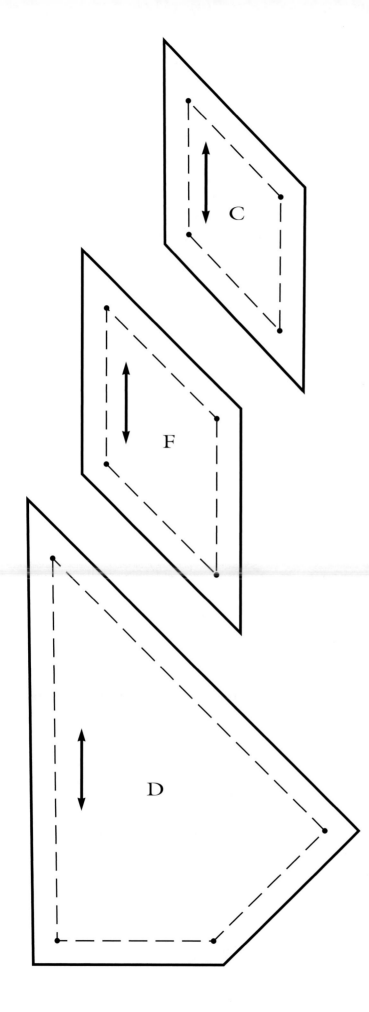

Honors and Awards

Within just one year of its completion in 2000, the Feathered Star won awards and special recognitions in 10 areas.

Machine Quilter's Showcase 2000: 2nd Place in heirloom category and Viewer's Choice

North Pittsburgh Quilt Guild Show 2000: Best of Show, Viewer's Choice, and Best Machine Quilting award

Three Rivers Quilt Show 2000: 3rd Place and Viewer's Choice

Canfield Fair 2000: Best of Show

Unlimited Possibilities: (trade newsletter for machine quilters) cover of July 2000 issue; cover photo and article in January 2001 issue

NQA (National Quilt Association) National Show 2001: Second Place

Beaver Valley Piecemakers Quilt Guild Show 2001: 1st Place and Best Machine Quilting

The Quilting Quarterly: Fall 2001 issue, photo published in the parade of award winners

2001 International Quilt Festival: featured in the Longarm Luminaries exhibit during quilt market and festival

Machine Quilter's Showcase 2001: Photos used in magazine advertising the 2001 showcase

Sandy Crawford
Boulder City, Nevada

*S*andy Crawford took her first quilting class in January 1996. Her neighbor, Susanne McGlone, taught the class and introduced her to the Boulder City Cut-Ups, a group that meets twice a month for all-day sewing.

"In the class, we were supposed to make a small wall hanging," says Sandy. "I went home and made a queen-size quilt and then hand-quilted it!"

Since then, Sandy has completed four more queen-size quilts, with others in progress. One completed quilt has 44,050 pieces and won Viewer's Choice at her guild's 2001 show. "That's the only quilt I've had commercially quilted," says Sandy. "I named the quilt *Pure Love*, a.k.a. *The Crazy Lady Quilt*."

"Quilting has pretty much become my life. It's pure therapy!"

"Quilting has pretty much become my life," Sandy confesses. "It's pure therapy! I dream about quilting, and my fingers are calloused to prove that I hand-quilt almost all my quilts."

In addition to her own masterpieces, Sandy has made quite a few quilts for various charities, including the Ronald McDonald House, Nathan Adelson Hospice, and fund-raising quilts for breast cancer research. Her devotion to others in her community may be best exemplified by the *God Bless America* quilt, which she designed for the new Nevada Veterans Nursing Home in Boulder City.

God Bless America
2001

While plans were underway for a new veterans' home in Boulder City, Nevada, director Jon Sias asked several quilt groups to make large flag wall quilts for permanent display in each of the four visitor areas. Sandy Crawford volunteered her group, the Boulder City Cut-Ups, to make one.

Sandy designed the pattern and did all the piecing and basting. Her friends helped complete the hand quilting, including adding pearl cotton to stitch the words, "God Bless America" into the quilt.

The newly finished quilt appeared in the 2001 "America: From the Heart" exhibit at the International Quilt Festival in Houston, Texas. This exhibit featured quilts made by people all over the world in response to the tragedies of September 11.

The quilt was returned by Veteran's Day, November 11, 2001. On that day, a flag presentation and dedication ceremony took place at the Veterans Cemetery. The event drew over 500 attendees, including former Nevada governor and *News* publisher Mike O'Callaghan, the keynote speaker. Mayor Bob Ferraro presented certificates of appreciation to 21 survivors of Pearl Harbor. The quilters presented Jon Sias with the finished quilts for the Veterans Nursing Home.

"Our veterans mean so much to us," says Sandy. "God bless and protect all involved in this new war."

God Bless America

Finished Size
Quilt: 81" x 54½"

Materials
¼ yard each of 6 assorted blue
    prints, light to dark
½ yard each of 6 assorted red
    prints, light to dark
½ yard each of 6 white and cream
    prints, light to dark
5 yards backing fabric
Twin-size batting

Cutting
Number fabrics 1–6 from lightest
to darkest.

From blue prints, cut:
- Fabric 1—1 (4" x 28½") strip.
- Fabric 2—3 (2½" x 28½") strips.
- Fabric 3—3 (2½" x 28½") strips.
- Fabric 4—3 (2½" x 28½") strips.
- Fabric 5—3 (2½" x 28½") strips.
- Fabric 6—1 (4" x 28½") strip
  and 1 (2½" x 28½") strip.

From red prints, cut:
- Fabric 1—2 (4½" x 42")
  strips. Cut strips into
  7 (2½" x 4½") rectangles and
  17 (4" x 4½") rectangles.
- Fabric 2—3 (4½" x 42") strips.
  Cut strips into 37 (2½" x 4½")
  rectangles.
- Fabric 3—3 (4½" x 42") strips.
  Cut strips into 37 (2½" x 4½")
  rectangles.
- Fabric 4—3 (4½" x 42") strips.
  Cut strips into 37 (2½" x 4½")
  rectangles.
- Fabric 5—3 (4½" x 42") strips.
  Cut strips into 37 (2½" x 4½")
  rectangles.

- Fabric 6—2 (4½" x 42") strips.
  Cut strips into 3 (2½" x 4½")
  rectangles and 17 (4" x 4½")
  rectangles.
- From all remainder, cut 8
  (2¼"-wide) strips for binding.

From white to cream prints, cut:
- Fabric 1—2 (4½" x 42") strips.
  Cut strips into 6 (2½" x 4½")
  rectangles and 15 (4" x 4½")
  rectangles.
- Fabric 2—3 (4½" x 42") strips.
  Cut strips into 33 (2½" x 4½")
  rectangles.
- Fabric 3—3 (4½" x 42") strips.
  Cut strips into 33 (2½" x 4½")
  rectangles.
- Fabric 4—3 (4½" x 42") strips.
  Cut strips into 33 (2½" x 4½")
  rectangles.
- Fabric 5—3 (4½" x 42") strips.
  Cut strips into 33 (2½" x 4½")
  rectangles.
- Fabric 6—2 (4½" x 42") strips.
  Cut strips into 3 (2½" x 4½")
  rectangles and 15 (4" x 4½")
  rectangles.

- From all remainder, cut 13 stars.

Quilt Assembly
1. Referring to *Quilt Top Assembly
Diagram*, join Fabric 6 red and
cream 2½" x 4½" rectangles with
blue 2½" x 28½" Fabric 6 strip to
make first row.

2. Repeat for next row, using
Fabric 5 pieces. Continue in this
manner to make rows from Fabrics
4, 3, and 2.

3. Referring to *Quilt Top Assembly
Diagram*, join Fabric 1 red and
white 4" x 4½" rectangles with
blue 4" x 28½" Fabric 1 strip.
Then proceed with smaller pieces
to make rows in Fabrics 2, 3, 4,
and 5.

4. Follow remainder of *Quilt Top
Assembly Diagram* closely to make
remainder of rows.

5. Join rows as shown in *Quilt Top
Assembly Diagram*, offsetting each
row by ½".

6. Appliqué 13 stars in blue area
as shown in photo.

Quilting and Finishing

1. Divide backing fabric into 2 (2½-yard) lengths. Cut 1 panel in half lengthwise. Sew 1 narrow panel to each side of wide panel. Press seam allowances toward narrow panels. Seams will run horizontally.

2. Layer backing, batting, and quilt top; baste. Quilt as desired. Quilt shown is outline-quilted around stars and in waves through stripe backgrounds. Stripes feature the words "God Bless America" in contrasting thread.

3. Join 2¼"-wide red strips into 1 continuous piece for straight-grain French-fold binding. Add binding to quilt, trimming excess from top and bottom before turning binding to back of quilt.

Star Template

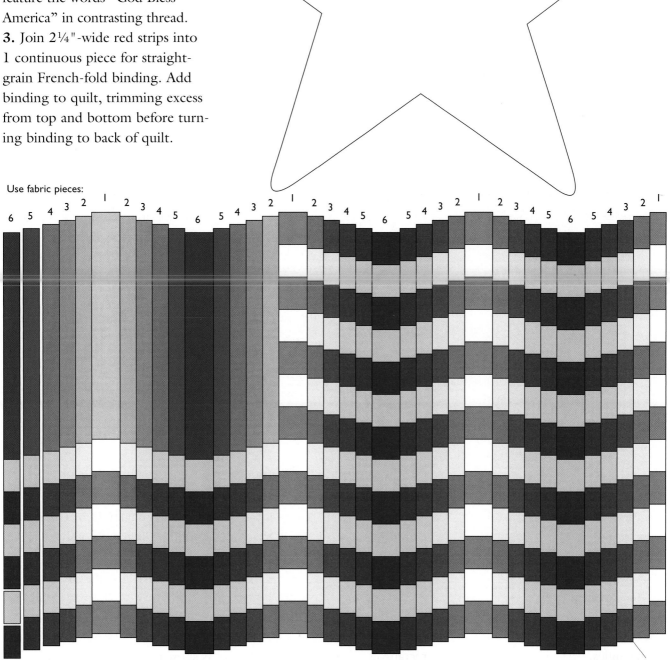

Use fabric pieces:

Quilt Top Assembly Diagram

Offset each row by ½".

On November 11, 2001, several members of the Boulder City Cut-Ups presented their quilt to Jon Sias, director of the new Nevada Veterans Nursing Home, where it will be on permanent display.

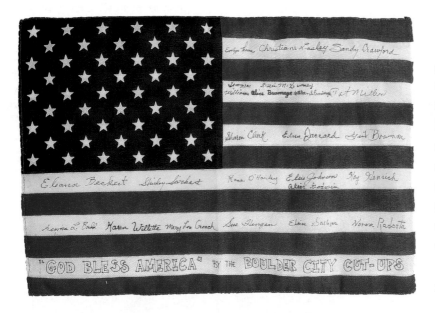

Quilt Label

To commemorate their group effort, Sandy Crawford found a piece of fabric that was printed with large flags. Each person who contributed to the project signed her name in a white stripe. The bottom white stripe indicates the name of the quilt and the name of the group.

See the facing page for more quilt label ideas.

Contributors

Boulder City Cut-Ups who contributed to hand-quilting *God Bless America* include:

Eleanor Beckert	Peg Cummings	Lu Hooker	Norma Radosta
Gail Bowman	Claudette Davison	Edna Jarrard	Naomi Rigas
Alice Brumage	Grace Deardoff	Elsie Johnson	Jolene Smalley
Georgia Budd	Kathleen Ernsberger	Ev Kleindler	Shirley Swihart
Sharon Clark	Elaine Gallegos	Christiane Lasley	Evelyn Thomas
Sandy Crawford	Alice Godwin	Dottie McKerney	Karen Willette
Mary Lou Creech	Sue Hengen	Pat Miller	Ida Mae Williams
Joyce Cucullu	Kay Henrich	Rose O'Hanley	

Quilt Labels

Every quilt you make should include a quilt label.
You can appliqué or piece the label to the back, or include
the information in a quilt block on the front.

At minimum, your quilt label should include the name of the quilt, your name, your city and state, and the date of completion or the date of presentation. Additional information can include the story behind the quilt, the maker, and/or the recipient.

There are numerous ways to embellish your quilt label. You can use Pigma® pens, rubber stamps, cross-stitch, embroidery, or even your computer. If a quilt label is designed on your computer, you can make a quilt label with photo transfer paper or with Computer Printer Fabric™ by June Tailor. Instructions come with the package. You can add more labels if the quilt is displayed, published, or acknowledged with an award. Shown on this page are examples of quilt labels from quilts featured in this book.

Irene Barker, maker of Fantastic 4th *on page 134, also enjoys embroidery. She stitched a patriotic picture from a sampler and made it into a quilt label. She added the explanation, "This quilt came off the frame July 4, 2000—hence the name."*

The Out of Towners, makers of the Sunday Quilt *featured on the cover and on page 88, used their computer to make a unique label. They live near a popular tourist town, Gatlinburg, Tennessee. They went to a specialty photo shop there that takes photos of their customers in period costumes. The women dressed up and had themselves photographed with the quilt. They scanned that image into their computer and produced a quilt label that documented their names and the reason for making the quilt.*

Trace, scan, or photocopy this quilt label to finish your quilt.

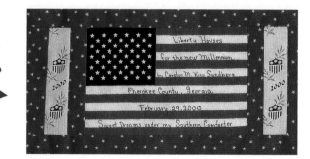

Carolyn Sundberg, maker of Liberty Houses *on page 14, found a small flag print for her quilt label. Like the Boulder City Cut-Ups shown on the facing page, she recorded her information on the white stripes. She added a commemorative conversation print to each side of the flag that notes the year was 2000.*

Sammie Simpson
Murphy, North Carolina

Sammie Simpson has been hooked on quilting ever since she took her first class in 1983 in Birmingham, Alabama. Since she has had to move throughout the Southeast, she is a member of several quilting groups, including the East Cobb Quilt Guild in Marietta, Georgia; the Bulloch Hall Quilt Guild in Roswell, Georgia; and A Gathering of Quilters in Murphy, North Carolina.

"I quilt every day, both by hand and by machine," says Sammie. "I like to do my hand quilting while watching television at night. I also enjoy teaching others what I have learned. I teach once a year at the John Campbell Folk School in Brasstown, North Carolina."

"I quilt every day, both by hand and by machine."

Sammie was also instrumental in the Olympic Games quilting project. She helped make *A Quilt of Leaves* for the 1996 Olympic Games in Atlanta, as well as the quilt that was sent to Nagano, Japan, for their games in 1998.

Sammie's Star
2001

"I always like to make something special for the East Cobb Quilt Show that takes place every other year in Marietta, Georgia," says Sammie. "I love old quilts, and I became particularly inspired by two-color quilts."

The traditional Feathered Star pattern allowed Sammie the empty background space she needed to showcase her machine quilting skills. After drafting the star to the size she wanted, Sammie drew her own quilting patterns to fill the empty areas.

"After I drafted the designs on paper, it took me over a week to transfer the designs on the quilt top," says Sammie. "The machine quilting took me about 70 hours, once I had everything layered and basted."

All of her hard work paid off. The quilt won "Best Machine Quilted" in the 2001 East Cobb Quilt Show.

Sammie's Star

Finished Size
Quilt: 101" x 101"

Materials
6 yards red
9½ yards white
9 yards backing fabric
King-size batting

Cutting
Instructions are for rotary cutting and quick piecing. Border strips are exact length needed. You may want to cut them longer to allow for piecing variations. Patterns are on page 35. **Cut pieces in order listed to make best use of yardage.**

From red, cut:
- 2 yards. Cut yardage into 4 (4½" x 66½") lengthwise strips for borders.
- From remainder, cut 4 (10⅞") squares. Cut squares in half diagonally to make 8 F triangles.
- 1 (22½") G square for center.
- 14 (2⅞" x 42") strips. Cut strips into 176 (2⅞") squares for As.
- 4 (2½") B squares.
- 8 Cs.
- 4 Ds.
- 4 (4") M squares.
- 16 Ks.
- 16 Ks reversed.
- 4 (3½") Q squares.
- 16 Os.
- 16 Os reversed.
- 11 (2¼" x 42") strips for binding.

From white, cut:
- 2 yards. Cut yardage into 4 (9" x 72") lengthwise strips for inner borders.

- 2½ yards. Cut yardage into 4 (10" x 82½") lengthwise outer border strips.
- 2 (13½" x 42") strips. Cut strips into 4 (13½") H squares.
- 1 (27½") square. Cut square in quarters diagonally to make 4 I triangles.
- 14 (2⅞" x 42") strips. Cut strips into 180 (2⅞") squares for As.
- 4 Es.
- 4 Es reversed.
- 2 (3½" x 42") strips. Cut strips into 16 (3½") L squares.
- 2 (3" x 42") strips. Cut strips into 16 (3") P squares.
- 16 Js.
- 16 Ns.

A Unit Assembly Diagram

Center Assembly
1. Referring to *A Unit Assembly Diagram*, draw a diagonal line from corner to corner on back of white 2⅞" squares. Place 1 red and 1 white square together, right sides facing. Stitch ¼" from line on both sides. Cut apart along drawn line and press open to make 2 A units. Make 344 A units.

2. Cut remaining A squares in half diagonally to make 8 red and 16 white A triangles.

3. Join 4 A units as shown in *Corner Set Diagram*. Add 1 white A triangle and 1 red C. Repeat.

4. Join 1 red B to 1 strip as shown to make 1 corner set. Make 4 corner sets (*Corner Set Diagram*).

Corner Set Diagram

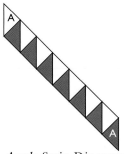

Angle Strip Diagram

5. Referring to *Angle Strip Diagram*, join 6 A units. Add 1 red and 1 white A triangle to each end as shown to make 1 angle strip. Make 8 angle strips, noting direction of angle.

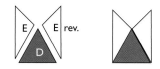

Star Joining Unit Diagram

6. Referring to *Star Joining Unit Diagram*, join 1 E and 1 E rev. to 1 D to make 1 star joining unit. Make 4 star joining units.

7. Referring to Top Unit of *Star Assembly Diagram*, lay out 2 corner sets, 2 angle strips, 2 F triangles, and 1 star joining unit. Join to make top unit. Repeat to make bottom unit.

8. Referring to *Star Assembly Diagram*, lay out 2 angle strips, 1 star joining unit, and 2 F triangles as shown. Join to make 1 side unit. Repeat for second side unit.

9. Referring to *Star Assembly Diagram*, lay out top, bottom, sides, and G square. Join to complete star.

10. Referring to *Quilt Top Assembly Diagram* on page 34, set in I triangles and H squares. Trim if needed, leaving ¼" seam allowance.

Border and Corner Block Assembly

Refer to *Quilt Top Assembly Diagram* as needed for borders.

1. To make pieced red borders, join 33 A units. Repeat. Join A unit strips to long sides of 1 red strip to make 1 red border strip. Make 4 red border strips.

2. To make outer corner star, join 1 K and 1 K rev. to 1 J triangle to make 1 side unit. Make 4 side units. Lay out 4 J/K side units, 1 M, and 4 Ls. Join to make 1 outer corner star block *(Outer Corner Star Block Diagram)*. Make 4 outer corner star blocks.

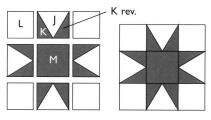

Outer Corner Star Block Diagram

3. To make inner corner star, join 1 O and 1 O rev. to 1 N triangle to make 1 side unit. Make 4 side units. Lay out 4 N/O side units, 1 Q, and 4 Ps. Join to make 1 inner corner star block *(Inner Corner Star Block Diagram)*. Make 4 inner corner star blocks.

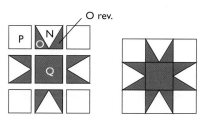

Inner Corner Star Block Diagram

Quilt Assembly

1. Referring to *Quilt Top Assembly Diagram*, center 1 white 9"-wide border strip on each side of star. Add to quilt, mitering corners. Trim evenly to 66½" x 66½".

2. Add 1 red border strip to opposite sides of center. Join 1 inner corner star block to each end of remaining red border

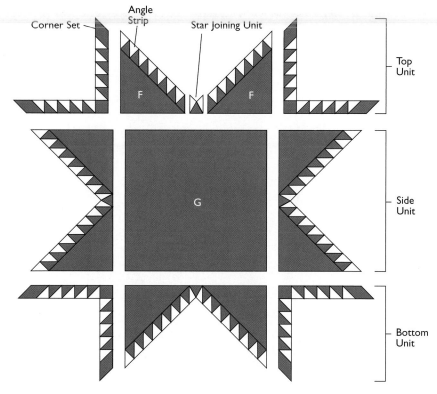

Star Assembly Diagram

strips. Add to top and bottom of center.

3. Join 1 white 10"-wide border strip to opposite sides of quilt. Join 1 outer corner star block to each end of remaining white border strips. Add to top and bottom of quilt.

Quilting and Finishing

1. Divide backing fabric into 3 (3-yard) lengths. Join panels to make backing; seams will run horizontally.

2. Layer backing, batting, and quilt top; baste. Quilt as desired. Quilt shown is heavily quilted in feathers, stars, florals, and ropes.

3. Join 2¼"-wide red strips into 1 continuous piece for straight-grain French-fold binding. Add binding to quilt.

Trace, scan, or photocopy this quilt label to finish your quilt.

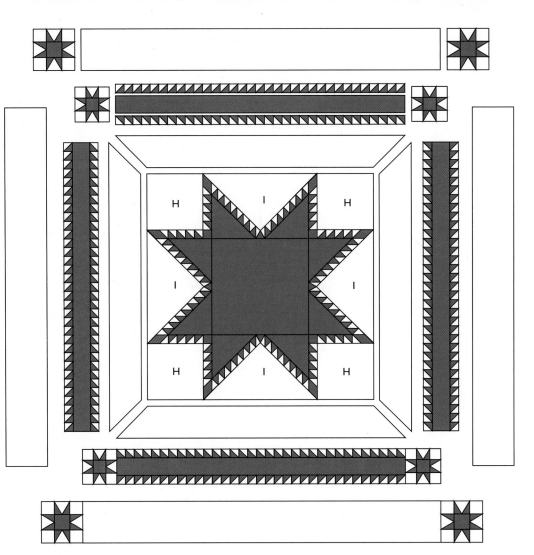

Quilt Top Assembly Diagram

34

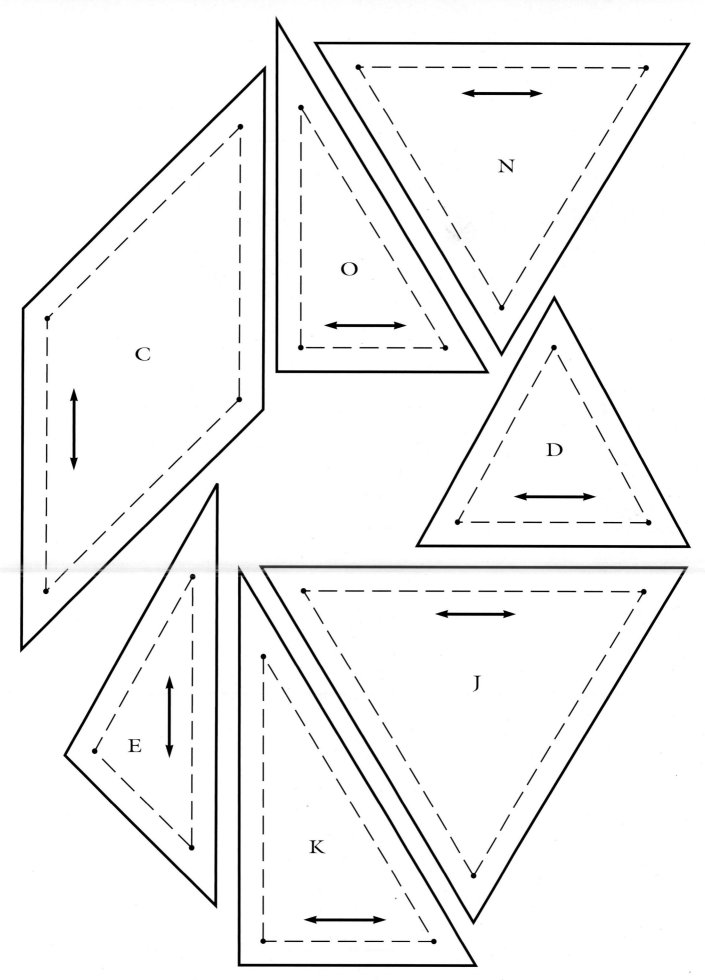

36

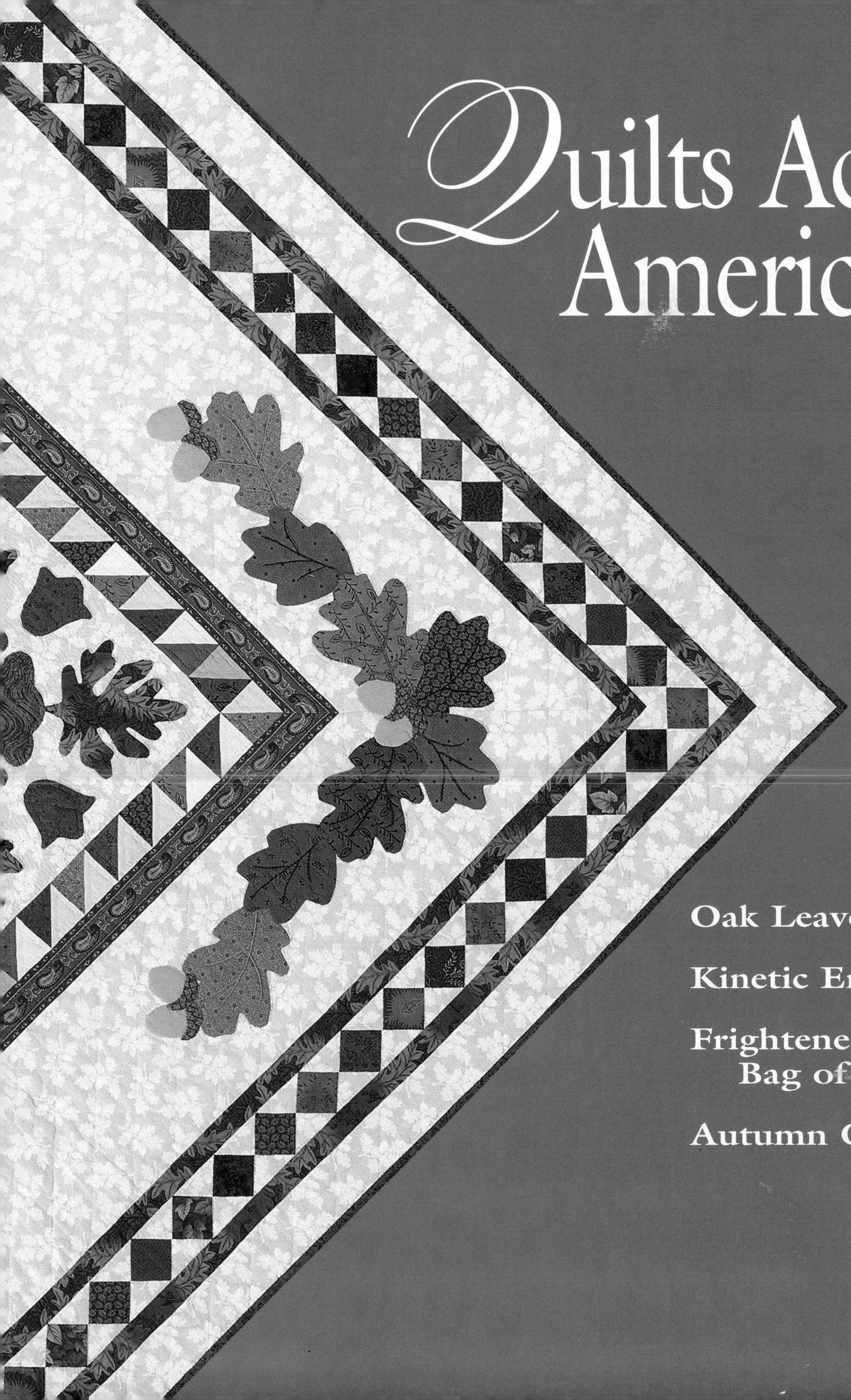

Quilts Across America

Oak Leaves & Anvil

Kinetic Energy

Frightened by a
Bag of M&M's®

Autumn Oaks Plaid

Gloria Greenlee
Cheyenne, Wyoming

Although Gloria Greenlee began quilting in 1984, she has been sewing since she was only eight. She began collecting fabric at age 12 and hasn't stopped since! It comes as no surprise that her favorite quilts are scrap quilts.

Gloria belongs to many quilting organizations, including the Cheyenne Heritage Quilters, the Green Country Quilters, the Wyoming State Quilters Group, the Oklahoma Quilters State Organization, the Colorado Quilt Council, the American Quilter's Society, and the International Quilt Association. She also finds time to participate in small stitching groups.

"...I usually have six different [quilts] in progress at the same time."

"I work on some quilt project almost every day, and I usually have at least six different ones in progress at the same time," Gloria confesses. "Quilting gives me the opportunity to play with color, design, and fabrics. Life is never boring because I get so wrapped up in my quilt projects."

Gloria sets aside a few quilts for herself, but generally, she gives them away. She has been teaching quilt classes since 1991, so she retains those she can use as teaching samples or ones that she cannot part with yet.

"I love traditional designs and antique quilts especially," says Gloria. "Scrappy quilts are my very special favorites."

Oak Leaves and Anvil
2000

Gloria has always loved quilts, but she didn't inherit any. She wanted to make some for herself and some to pass down to her children. She also began scouring estate sales to find antique quilts for her collection.

It was at such a sale that she found inspiration for *Oak Leaves and Anvil*. She based her quilt's block design on an antique block pattern she discovered and then designed the setting and the borders.

The quilt has been exhibited at the 2001 National Quilting Association show and at the 2001 Quilting in the Tetons show. It won blue ribbons in

both the Laramie County Fair of 2001 and the Wyoming State Fair in 2001.

Oak Leaves and Anvil

Finished Size

Quilt: 72" x 72"

Blocks: 4 (16" x 16")

Materials

5 yards cream-on-tan print for background and borders

1 fat quarter (18" x 22") dark brown print for appliqué

1 fat quarter (18" x 22") rust brown print for appliqué

4 fat eighths (9" x 22") blue prints for appliqué and diamonds

1½ yards blue-and-brown print for oak leaves and borders

10 fat eighths (9" x 22") assorted rust brown prints for sashing and leaves

8 (3" x 22") strips assorted solid cream to light brown fabrics for sashing

1¼ yard blue-and-rust paisley stripe for inner border

1 fat eighth (9" x 22") light brown for acorns

1 (3" x 22") strip brown print for acorn caps

¾ yard blue print for binding

4½ yards backing fabric

Full-size batting

Coordinating floss for leaf veins

Cutting

Instructions are for rotary cutting and quick piecing. Border strips are exact length needed. You may want to cut them longer to allow for piecing variations. You may use scraps for greater variety for diamond border, sashing, and leaves. Patterns are on pages 42–43. **Cut pieces in order listed to make best use of yardage.**

From cream-on-tan print, cut:

- 1¾ yards. Cut yardage into 4 (9" x 63") lengthwise appliqué border strips.
- 2⅛ yards. Cut yardage into 4 (3" x 76½") lengthwise outer border strips and 4 (17") squares for appliqué.
- 5 (3¾" x 42") strips. Cut strips into 48 (3¾") squares. Cut squares in quarters diagonally to make 192 side triangles for diamond border.
- 1 (2⅛" x 42") strip. Cut strips into 8 (2⅛") squares. Cut squares in half diagonally to make 16 corner triangles for diamond border.

From dark brown print, cut:

- 4 Ds.

From rust brown print, cut:

- 16 Fs. Remainder may be used for sashing units.

From blue prints, cut:

- 4 As and 16 Bs from 1 print.
- 16 Cs from darker print.
- 100 (2¼") squares for diamond border from all prints.

From blue-and-brown print, cut:

- 14 (1½" x 42") strips. Piece strips to make 2 (1½" x 58½") inner side borders, 2 (1½" x 60½") inner top and bottom borders, 2 (1½" x 65½") outer side borders, and 2 (1½" x 67½") outer top and bottom borders.
- 16 oak leaves (E).

From assorted rust brown prints, cut:

- 52 (2⅞") squares for sashing units.
- 16 oak leaves (G).
- 16 oak leaves (G rev.).

From assorted solid fabric strips, cut:

- 1 (2½") square for center.
- 52 (2⅞") squares for sashing units.

From blue-and-rust paisley stripe, cut:
- 4 (2" x 45") lengthwise strips for border, centered on stripe.

From light brown, cut:
- 24 acorns (H).

From brown print, cut:
- 24 acorn caps (I).

From blue print, cut:
- 8 (2¼" x 42") strips for binding.

Block Assembly

1. Clip a small hole in center of A, B, and C placements on 1 D piece. Baste A, B, and C pieces in place on back of D, right side of blue against wrong side of brown. Reverse appliqué A, Bs, and Cs. Remove basting.

2. Fold 1 (17") square in quarters and press, both straight and diagonally, to make appliqué guidelines *(Folding Diagram)*. Arrange 1 D, 4 Es, and 4 Fs on square. Appliqué in place. Trim block evenly to 16½" x 16½" to complete 1 appliqué block *(Block Diagram)*.

Folding Diagram

2. Make 4 appliqué blocks.

Block Diagram

Sashing Unit Assembly Diagram

Sashing Assembly

1. Referring to *Sashing Unit Assembly Diagram*, draw a diagonal line from corner to corner on back of solid 2⅞" squares. Place 1 solid and 1 rust brown print squares together, right sides facing. Stitch ¼" from line on both sides. Cut apart and press open to make 2 sashing units. Make 104 sashing units.

2. Join 8 sashing units to make 1 sashing strip *(Sashing Strip Diagram 1)*. Make 4 sashing strips.

Sashing Strip Diagram 1

Quilt Assembly

Refer to *Quilt Top Assembly Diagram* throughout.

1. Lay out blocks, sashing strips, and center sashing square. Join into rows; join rows to complete center.

2. Join 17 sashing units to make 1 side strip. Make 2 side strips. Join to center, noting direction of triangles.

3. Join 19 sashing units to make top strip, noting rotation of end unit *(Sashing Strip Diagram 2)*.

Quilt Top Assembly Diagram

Sashing Strip Diagram 2

Add to top of quilt. Repeat for bottom sashing strip.

4. Center 1 paisley strip on each side of quilt and add. Miter corners.

5. Center 1 (9"-wide) cream border strip on each side of quilt and add. Miter corners.

6. Appliqué 8 leaves, 6 acorns, and 6 caps on each corner of cream border. Refer to photo for placement. Stemstitch veins on leaves with coordinating floss.

7. Add blue inner side borders. Add blue inner top and bottom borders.

8. Referring to *Border Unit Assembly Diagram,* join 1 side triangle to opposite sides of 1 blue square to make 1 border unit. Make 92 border units.

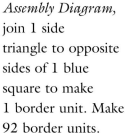

Border Unit Assembly Diagram

9. Join 22 border units as shown in *Border Assembly Diagram.* Join 1 square, 1 side triangle, and 2 corner triangles as shown to make end unit. Add to strip. Repeat for opposite end of strip to make 1 side diamond border. Check strip for fit; adjust if needed. Add to 1 side of quilt. Repeat for opposite side.

10. In a similar manner, join 24 border units. Join 1 square, 1 side triangle, and 2 corner triangles to make end unit. Add to strip. Repeat for opposite end of strip to make top diamond border. Check strip for fit; adjust if needed. Add to top of quilt. Repeat for bottom diamond border.

11. Add blue outer side borders. Add blue outer top and bottom borders.

12. Center 1 (3"-wide) border strip on each side of quilt and add. Miter corners.

Quilting and Finishing

1. Divide backing fabric into 2 (2¼-yard) lengths. Cut 1 piece in half lengthwise. Sew 1 narrow panel to each side of wide panel. Press seam allowances toward narrow panels.

2. Layer backing, batting, and quilt top; baste. Quilt as desired. Quilt shown is echo-quilted around appliqué in blocks. Triangles are outline-quilted, and background is diamond grid quilted, based on diamond border.

3. Join 2¼"-wide blue print strips into 1 continuous piece for straight-grain French-fold binding. Add binding to quilt.

F

E

Border Assembly Diagram

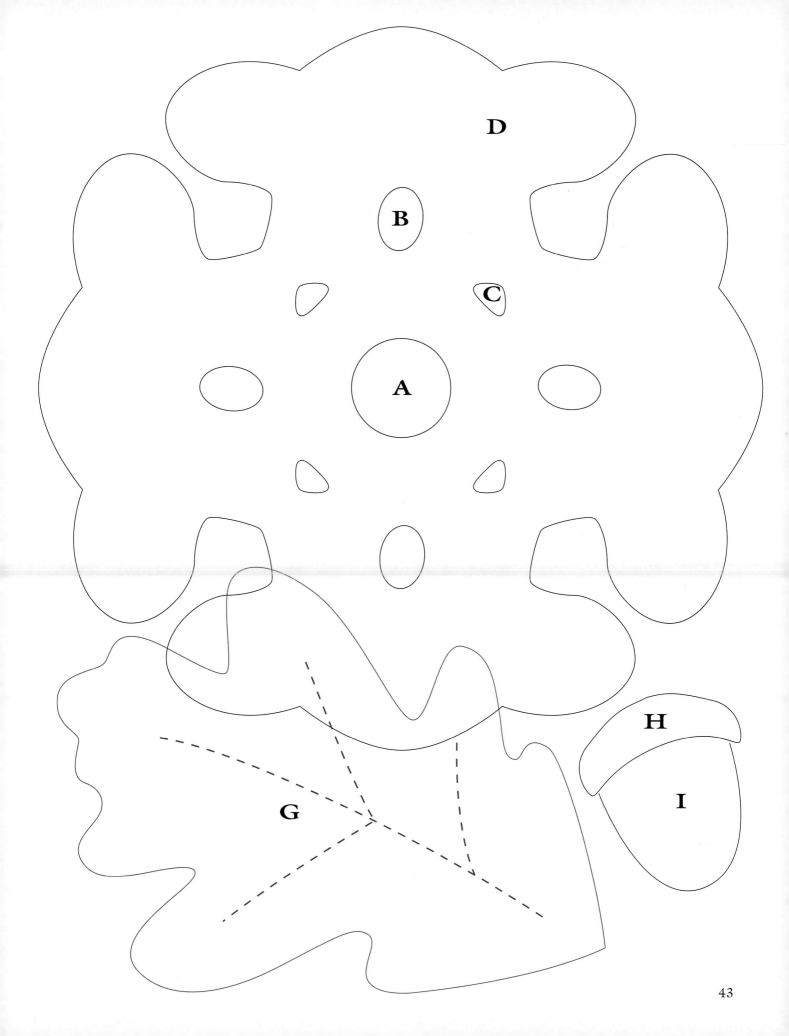

D

B

C

A

G

H

I

43

Ariel Alberga-Martin
Lansing, New York

Ariel Alberga-Martin has always had quilts in her life. "I was lucky to be born into a very creative family," says Ariel. "My mother, my grandmother, as well as various aunts and cousins, were all quilters." Ariel made her first quilt in her teens, under the guidance of her mother. When she started her own home with four young children, Ariel sold most of her quilts in shops. Now that she's retired, she takes time to make quilts for herself.

"I was lucky to be born into a very creative family,"

Ariel is is a member of the Tompkins County Quilt Guild in Ithaca, New York. She also participates in a spin-off group from the guild, the Contemporary Quilters. She's a long-distance member of the Cairo Piecemakers, who meet monthly in Cairo, New York. In addition to her work with these groups, Ariel quilts one morning a week with the Lansing Quilters at the Lansing United Methodist Church. "We do quilting for other people—quilting new tops they've made or old ones they'd like finished," says Ariel. "The money earned goes to various community and church needs."

"To me, creating with fabric is a means of self-expression."

Having quilted for more than 40 years, quilting permeates every area of Ariel's life. "I observe an object, an event, or hear a phrase, and my mind translates it into fabric," says Ariel. "My sketch book goes everywhere with me so I can keep track of my ideas. To me, creating with fabric is a means of self-expression."

Kinetic Energy
1999

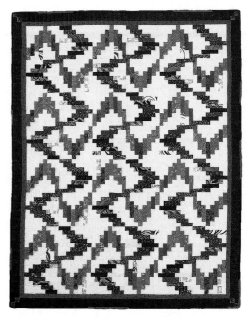

Kinetic Energy is the result of a challenge that Ariel set for herself to make a quilt using only three colors—a radical departure from her "the-more-color-the-better" approach to quiltmaking.

"I alleviated the stress of this three-color limitation by using a variety of reds, blacks, and whites," says Ariel. "The reds and blacks came from my shelves. I seldom use white in my work, so I purchased those fabrics specifically for this quilt."

In science, kinetic energy is energy associated with motion. Ariel's use of fabric certainly conveys this idea in her work. The black and red fabrics seem to create waving lines of energy across the quilt. The bold colors sizzle against the stark background. The fabrics keep the eye moving.

Kinetic Energy

Finished Size
Quilt: 67½" x 87½"
Blocks: 12 (20" x 20")

Materials
12 fat quarters (18" x 22") assorted white and cream prints for blocks

7 fat quarters (18" x 22") assorted red prints for blocks

7 fat quarters (18" x 22") assorted black prints for blocks

¾ yard red print for border and binding

1½ yards black print for border and binding

5½ yards backing fabric

Twin-size batting

Cutting
Instructions are for rotary cutting and quick piecing. Border strips are exact length needed. You may want to cut them longer to allow for piecing variations. **Cut pieces in order listed to make best use of yardage.**

From white and cream prints, cut:
- 4 (6¾" x 22") strips.
- 12 (5½" x 22") strips.
- 8 (4¼" x 22") strips.
- 16 (3" x 22") strips.
- 12 (1¾" x 22") strips.

From red prints, cut:
- 10 (5½" x 22") strips.
- 6 (4¼" x 22") strips.
- 2 (1¾" x 22") strips.
- 1 (1¾" x 22") strip for corner Four-Patch blocks.

From black prints, cut:
- 10 (5½" x 22") strips.
- 6 (4¼" x 22") strips.
- 2 (1¾" x 22") strips.

From red print, cut:
- 8 (1¾" x 42") strips. Piece strips to make 2 (1¾" x 80½") side borders and 2 (1¾" x 63") top and bottom borders.
- 2 (2¼" x 42") strips. Cut strips into random lengths from 5" to 12" long for binding.

From black print, cut:
- 8 (3" x 42") strips. Piece to make 2 (3" x 83") side borders and 2 (3" x 63") top and bottom borders.
- 1 (1¾" x 42") strip. Trim strip to 1¾" x 22" for corner Four-Patch block strip.
- 7 (2¼" x 42") strips for binding.

Block Assembly
Refer to *Strip Set Assembly Diagrams* throughout.

1. Join 1 red 4¼" x 22" strip and 1 white 6¾" x 22" strip to make 1 Strip Set A. Make 2 Strip Sets A. Cut strip set into 24 (1¾"-wide) A segments.

2. Join 1 white 1¾" strip, 1 red 4¼" strip, and 1 white 5½" strip to make 1 Strip Set B. Make 2 Strip Sets B. Cut strip sets into 24 (1¾"-wide) B segments.

3. Join 1 white 3" strip, 1 red 5½" strip, and 1 white 3" strip to make 1 Strip Set C. Make 4 Strip Sets C. Cut strip sets into 48 (1¾"-wide) C segments.

4. Join 1 white 4¼" strip, 1 red 5½" strip, and 1 white 1¾" strip to make 1 Strip Set D. Make 4 Strip Sets D. Cut strip sets into 48 (1¾"-wide) D segments.

5. Join 1 white 5½" strip and 1 red 5½" strip to make 1 Strip Set E. Make 2 Strip Sets E. Cut strip sets into 24 (1¾"-wide) E segments.

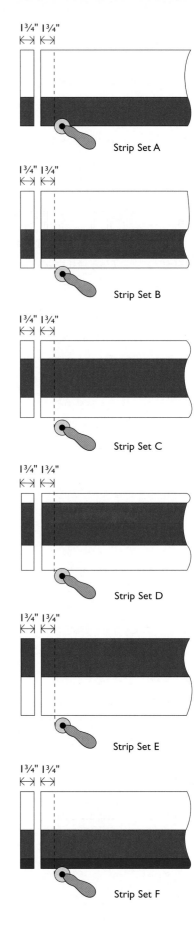

Strip Set Assembly Diagrams

6. Join 1 red 1¾" strip, 1 red 4¼" strip and 1 white 5½" strip to make 1 Strip Set F. Make 2 Strip Sets F. Cut strip set into 24 (1¾"-wide) F segments.

7. Referring to *Unit Assembly Diagram,* lay out in order 1 each of segments A, B, C, D, E, D, C, and F. Check position of strips. Join to make 1 red unit (*Unit Diagram*). Make 24 red units.

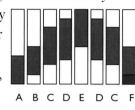

Unit Assembly Diagram

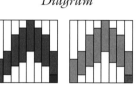

Unit Diagram

8. Repeat Steps 1–7 to make 24 black units, replacing red strips in strip sets with equal width black strips.

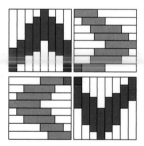

Block Assembly Diagram

9. Lay out 2 red and 2 black units, rotating as shown in *Block Assembly Diagram.* Join to make 1 block (*Block Diagram*). Make 12 blocks.

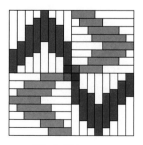

Block Diagram

Quilt Assembly

1. Lay out blocks as shown in *Quilt Top Assembly Diagram.* Join into rows; join rows to complete quilt center.

2. Add red side borders to quilt. Add red top and bottom borders to quilt.

3. Referring to *Four-Patch Assembly Diagram,* join 1 red and 1 black 1¾" x 22" strips to make 1 strip set. Cut strip set into 8 (1¾"-wide) segments. Join 2 segments to make 1 corner Four-Patch. Make 4 Four-Patch blocks.

Four-Patch Assembly Diagram

4. Add black side borders to quilt. Join 1 Four-Patch block to each end of remaining borders, rotating as shown. Add to top and bottom of quilt.

Quilting and Finishing

1. Divide backing fabric into 2 (2¾-yard) lengths. Cut 1 piece in half lengthwise. Sew 1 narrow panel to each side of wide panel. Press seam allowances toward narrow panels.

2. Layer backing, batting, and quilt top; baste. Quilt as desired. Quilt shown is machine-quilted in waves through black and red areas. Light areas are meander-quilted. Borders have parallel lines extended from blocks.

3. Join 2¼"-wide black and red strips into 1 continuous piece for straight-grain French-fold binding, placing red strips in at random. Add binding to quilt.

Quilt Top Assembly Diagram

Bette Lee Collins
Red Bluff, California

Bette Lee Collins of Red Bluff, California, inherited her love of handwork and sewing from her mother and grandmother. "When my mom made a Sunbonnet Sue baby quilt for my daughter, my interest in quilting was rekindled. Each time I put a stitch in a quilt, I honor them both."

Although she made her first quilt in the 1970s, her quilting took off in earnest in the 1980s after attending her first quilt show. "I soon began entering my quilts in shows, and that led to teaching classes, judging shows, and conducting workshops and lectures with my friend, Babs Robinson," says Bette Lee. "Our goal is to continue quilting until we're ready for the 'quilter's retirement home!' We love sharing, and the sharing we receive from our students is a wonderful bonus."

Bette Lee is active in her local quilting community, serving as Founding Member, Vice-President, and Quilt Show Co-Chair for the *"The joy of quilting is in the discovery."* Sun Country Quilters in Red Bluff and other posts in the Quilter's Sew-Ciety of Redding, California. She is also a member of national organizations such as the American Quilter's Society, the National Quilters Society, and the International Quilters Society.

"I like the surprises the quiltmaking process brings—not having enough fabric, finding one block that doesn't fit quite right, or deciding to make the quilt bigger as I go along," explains Bette Lee. "The joy of quilting is in the discovery."

Frightened by a Bag of M&M's®
2000

While making this quilt, Bette Lee Collins accidentally spilled a bag of M&M's candy across the quilt top. Luckily, the milk chocolate melts in your mouth, not on your quilt—but the incident gave her the idea for the quilt's clever name. It also led to the whimsical dots appliquéd across the quilt top.

This quilt has won many honors:
• First Place in "Color: Effective Use of Color and Design" at the 31st Annual National Quilt Association Quilt Show in Reno, Nevada, 2000
• First Place and $500 for Best Use of Color at the 2000 World Quilt and Textile Tour
• Cover quilt project for *Fons and Porter's For the Love of Quilting* magazine, July/August 2001
• Juried into the American Quilter's Association Quilt Show in Paducah, Kentucky, 2000
• Exhibited at the Road to California show in 2001

Frightened by a Bag of M&M's

Finished Size
Quilt: 82" x 94"
Blocks: 20 (10" x 10")

Materials
40 fat quarters (18" x 22") assorted hand-dyed fabrics for blocks, sashing, and pieced borders
½ yard yellow for inner border
¾ yard tangerine for middle border
¾ yard black for outer border
¾ yard brown for binding
5½ yards backing fabric
Queen-size batting

Cutting
Instructions are for rotary cutting and quick piecing. Patterns are on page 51. **Cut pieces in order listed to make best use of yardage.**

From each of 40 fat quarters, cut:
- 1 (2½" x 22") strip for A units (total of 40).
- 2 (2½" x 22") strips for pieced borders (total of 80).

From remainder of 25 fat quarters, cut from each:
- 1 (2½" x 22") strip. Cut strip into 2 (2½" x 10½") sashing strips (total of 49).
- 1 (2½" x 22") strip. Cut strip into 1 (2½" x 10½") C rectangle and 2 (2½" x 4½") B rectangles (total of 20 sets).
- 1 D circle (total of 20).
- 1 E circle (total of 12).
- 2 (2½") squares for sashing squares and yellow border corners (total of 34).

From yellow, cut:
- 6 (2½" x 42") strips. Piece to make 2 (2½" x 50½") top and bottom strips and 2 (2½" x

62½") side strips for first unpieced border.

From tangerine, cut:
- 7 (2½" x 42") strips. Piece to make 2 (2½" x 62½") top and bottom strips and 2 (2½" x 70½") side strips for second solid border.

From black, cut:
- 9 (2½" x 42") strips. Piece to make 2 (2½" x 82½") top and bottom strips and 2 (2½" x 90½") side strips for outer border.

From brown, cut:
- 10 (2¼" x 42") strips for binding.

Block Assembly
1. Choose 2 different A strips, 1 set of 2 B rectangles and 1 matching C rectangle, plus 1 D circle.

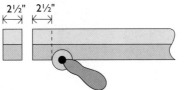

Strip Set Diagram

2. Referring to *Strip Set Diagram*, join A strips on long sides. Press seam allowance to one side. Cut strip into 8 (2½"-wide) A segments. Join 2 A segments as shown in *Four-Patch Assembly Diagram* to make 1 A unit. Make 4 A units.

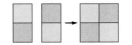

Four-Patch Assembly Diagram

3. Referring to *Block Assembly Diagram*, lay out A units, B rectangles, and C rectangle as shown. Join into rows; join rows to complete piecing.

4. Appliqué D circle in center to complete 1 block (*Block Diagram*). Make 20 blocks.

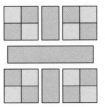
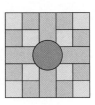

Block Assembly Diagram   *Block Diagram*

Pieced Border Assembly

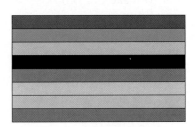

Border Strip Set Diagram

1. Referring to *Border Strip Set Diagram*, join 8 border strips to make 1 strip set. Make 10 strip sets.

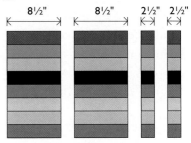

Border Cutting Diagram

2. Referring to *Border Cutting Diagram*, cut each strip set into 2 (8½"-wide) outer border segments and 2 (2½"-wide) inner border segments.

3. To make inner pieced border, join 4 (2½"-wide) segments end to end. Add 1 square from extra segment to make 1 (33-square) side inner border. Repeat for second side inner border.

4. Join 4 (2½"-wide) segments end to end. Remove 3 squares from end to make 1 (29-square) top inner border. Repeat to make bottom inner border.

5. To make side outer pieced

border, join 5 (8½"-wide) segments end to end. From 1 extra segment, remove 3 strips. Add remaining 5-strip segment to complete 1 (45-strip) side border. Repeat for second side border.

6. Join 4 (8½"-wide) segments end to end. Remove 1 strip from end to make 1 (31-strip) top border. Repeat to make bottom border.

Quilt Assembly

1. Lay out pieces as shown in *Quilt Top Assembly Diagram*. Join into rows; join rows to make quilt center. Appliqué 1 E circle over each inner sashing intersection (12 in all).

2. Add yellow side borders to quilt. Add 2½" squares to ends of remaining yellow borders. Add to top and bottom of quilt.

3. Add side inner pieced borders. Add top and bottom inner pieced borders

4. Add side tangerine borders. Add top and bottom tangerine borders.

5. Add top and bottom outer pieced borders. Add side outer pieced borders.

6. Add side black borders. Add top and bottom black borders.

Quilting and Finishing

1. Divide backing fabric into 2 (2¾-yard) lengths. Cut 1 piece in half lengthwise. Sew 1 narrow panel to each side of wide panel.

2. Layer backing, batting, and quilt top; baste. Quilt as desired. Quilt shown was quilted in overlapping bull's-eyes in center and in Baptist Fans in inner borders. Outer border has parallel quilting.

3. Join 2¼"-wide brown strips into 1 continuous piece for straight-grain French-fold binding. Add binding to quilt.

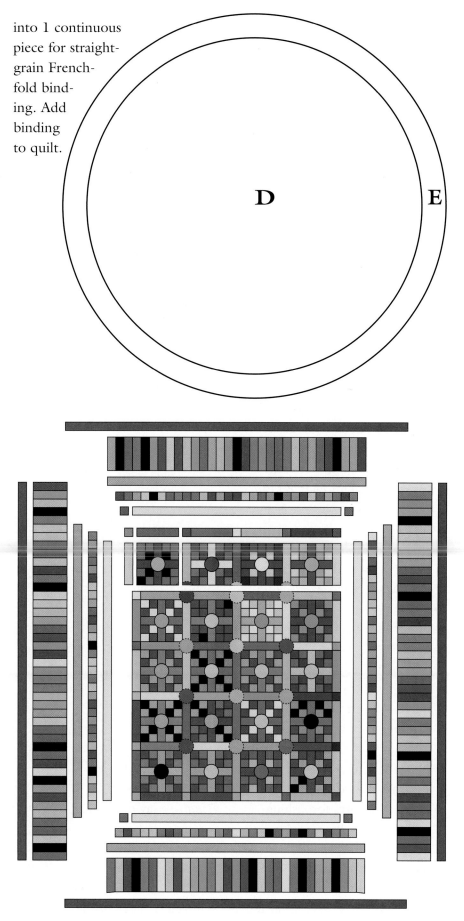

Quilt Top Assembly Diagram

Mickey Depre
Oak Lawn, Illinois

*M*ickey Depre began quilting in the 1980s. At the time, she enjoyed making traditional quilt patterns. However, she had to set her hobby aside when her twins were born in 1990. "I found my way back to quilting in 1996, when school sessions brought free time back to my days," says Mickey. "I will never leave again."

"My work is meant to spark the imagination and to bring a smile to a viewer's face."

Mickey's taste in textiles runs the gamut from vintage prints to contemporary hand-dyed fabrics. "When I pushed myself beyond traditional quiltmaking," Mickey says, "I found it very liberating and inviting. The images in my mind found their way into fiber."

Now an award-winning professional quilter, Mickey's work has appeared in many national juried shows, in magazines, and in books. "My work is meant to spark the imagination and to bring a smile to a viewer's face," says Mickey. "Humor is a great gift to share."

Autumn Oaks Plaid
2001

Autumn Oaks Plaid is an original design by Mickey Depre, which she made by combining commercial fabrics with her own hand-dyed fabrics.

Mickey enjoys the process of quiltmaking, and she conveys this enthusiasm to students who take her quilt classes. She likes to make the techniques fun, giving the quiltmaker freedom for creativity. In this quilt, for example, you'll find fused shapes and machine appliqué with both satin-stitching and exposed raw edges.

"This quilt is my celebration of the season," says Mickey. "The changing leaves, cool winds, and start of the school year spurred on a muse in my mind. I find autumn and its visual display to be both uplifting and calming at the same time."

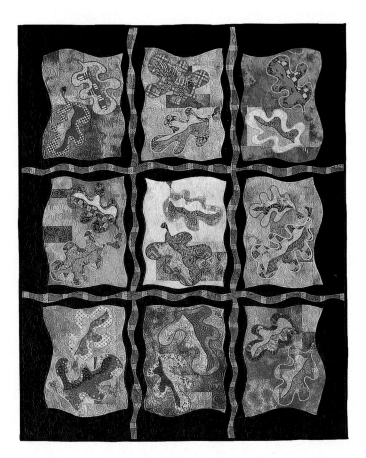

Autumn Oaks Plaid

Finished Size
Quilt: 33" x 42"
Blocks: 9 (11" x 14")

Materials
3 yards total fat quarters (18" x 22") and scraps assorted plaids, brights, batiks, and prints for blocks
Scraps of brown for leaf stems
1½ yards black for border and binding
1 (6" x 45") rectangle plaid for border (plaids often exceed 42" width)
1 yard backing fabric
Crib-size batting
Pellon Décor Bond® fusible adhesive
Pellon WonderUnder®
Heat-N-Bond® fusible webbing

Cutting
Block pieces are "cut as you go" due to the variety of blocks. Patterns are on page 56.
From black, cut:
• 1 (14" x 42") strip for inner borders.
• 2 (7" x 42") strips for outer borders.
• 4 (2¼" x 42") strips for binding.

General Block Assembly Instructions
See photograph for example.

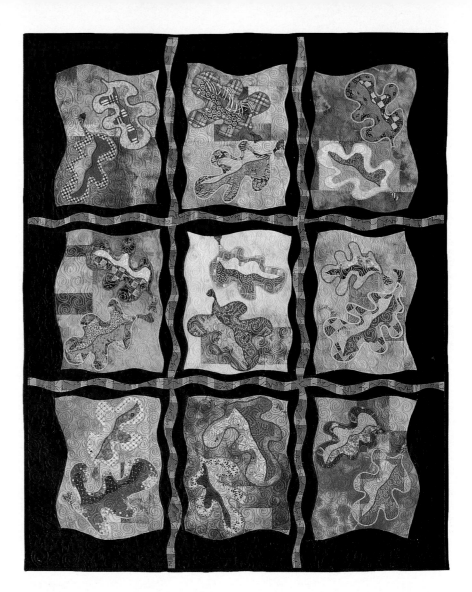

1. Referring to *Block Diagram,* join 4 (2¾" x 4") assorted rectangles to make 1 (5" x 7½") Four-Patch or "color window."

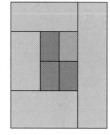

Block Diagram

Add random-width strips to each side to frame color window. Frame strips should be at least 3½" wide; framed size of block should be at least 11" x 14".

2. Adhere Décor Bond to back of block. Iron from front of block; Décor Bond will shrink and wrinkle under direct heat.

3. Leaf patterns are provided in two sizes as a general pattern. Vary leaves as desired. Trace leaf pattern onto non-bond side of Décor Bond. Bond to colorful fabric for leaf base. Cut out leaf on drawn line.

4. Trace center pieces of leaf on Pellon Wonder Under. Divide and bond to 2 different high-contrast fabrics. Cut out on lines. Remove paper backing and fuse to center of full leaf. Satin-stitch down center of leaf, covering edges, to define leaf vein.

5. Repeat for second leaf. Cut leaf stems from brown scraps fused to WonderUnder.

6. Place leaves on block, keeping at least 3" from edges. When satisfied with placement, fuse stem in place and satin-stitch appliqué leaves around outer edges. Trim background fabric from behind leaves.

7. Make 9 blocks, varying color window and color combinations as desired.

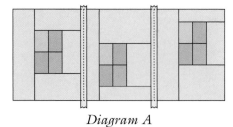

Diagram A

Quilt Assembly

1. Lay out blocks in 3 horizontal rows of 3 blocks each. When satisfied with placement, turn face down, preserving order. Tape together with 1"-wide masking tape along seam lines *(Diagram A)*. Carefully turn unit right side up.

2. Cut Décor Bond to fit 14" x 42" black strip. Fuse to back. Cut black strip into 4 (3½" x 42") strips. On back of each strip, mark ¾" in on each long edge *(Border Diagram 1)*. This is your guideline for cutting edges.

3. With a rotary cutter, cut soft waves along length of strips on both sides, staying within guidelines *(Border Diagram 1)*. Place strips over taped seams of blocks, adjusting so that leaves are not overlapped *(Diagram B)*. When satisfied with placement, remove lengthwise strips; pin widthwise strips in place and satin-stitch edges. Turn quilt and trim excess from behind widthwise strips (this removes widthwise tape also).

¾" 2" ¾"

Border Diagram 1

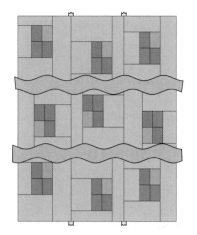

Diagram B

Repeat with lengthwise strips.

4. Cut Décor Bond to fit 2 (7" x 42") strips. Fuse to back as before. On Bond side, draw a center line, 3½" from each long edge *(Border Diagram 2)*. On each side of center line, draw another line 1" from center. Cut a centered wave between these two lines. Repeat with second strip for 4 outer border strips.

5. On Bond side of border strips, draw a line 1½" from straight edge for Nine-Patch placement. Align lengthwise borders with edge of blocks using guideline *(Diagram C)*. When satisfied with placement, pin and satin-stitch lengthwise edges. Trim excess from back. Repeat with top and bottom borders.

6. Fuse Heat-N-Bond to back of 6" x 45" plaid strip. Cut into

2½" 1" 1" 2½"

Border Diagram 2

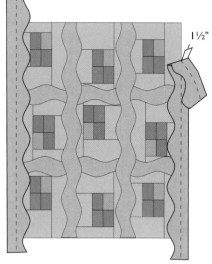

1½"

Diagram C

4 (1½" x 45") strips. Randomly cut waves on both sides of each strip. Position over black inner borders in a crosshatch pattern. When satisfied with placement, fuse in place. Trim excess from ends.

Quilting and Finishing

1. Layer backing, batting, and quilt top; baste.

2. Machine-quilt as desired. Quilt shown is machine-quilted in swirls using coordinating thread in blocks. Borders are quilted with black thread in swirls and jags.

3. Join 2¼"-wide black strips into 1 continuous piece for straight-grain French-fold binding. Add binding to quilt.

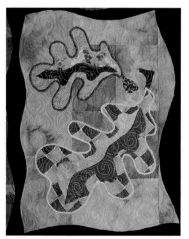

Small Leaf

Large Leaf

56

Fusible Facts

Fusible web, such as those made by Pellon and Heat-N-Bond, are heat-activated adhesives with a temporary paper lining. A hot iron melts the glue, fusing fabric shapes to the background material.

Choose the Correct Weight

Fusible web is available at fabric and craft stores off the bolt or in several pre-packaged widths and lengths.

- **Test different weights** to find the one that suits your project best. Generally, you can use regular weight web to make wall hangings, curtains, and other soft furnishings. Heavy-duty web is best for wood and cardboard projects.
- **For a garment,** heavy-duty web may add too much stiffness. Use regular weight web and finish the appliqué edges as necessary to ensure a washable wearable.
- **Read the package label** for tips on application and washability.
- **Test the product on scraps** of fabric before you start to appliqué. Let the sample cool, and then check to see that the fabric pieces have bonded and that the fused layers won't separate.

Be Prepared

Fusible appliqué is most fun when you don't encounter an unexpected complication or lack of materials in the middle of a project. Follow these suggestions to make your appliqué experience a pleasant one.

- **Keep these supplies on hand:** fabric marker, iron, ironing board, pressing cloth (one for fabric and one for paper), and fabrics.
- **Prewash all fabrics** to remove sizing, which prevents fusible web from bonding with fabric.
- **Experiment with fabrics.** Cotton works well with fusible appliqué, but you can also use more exotic fabrics, too. Be adventurous with lamé, cotton velvet and velveteen, faux suede, or corduroy. Some fabrics require care with application of heat and steam.
- **Avoid fusing** rayon, silk velvet, and rayon/acetate.
- **Use a damp pressing cloth.** The pressing cloth protects your iron and provides moisture to fuse the webbing to the fabric. It also acts as a temperature and timing guide. After holding the iron on the pressing cloth for 10–15 seconds, the cloth should be dry. If it is still damp, more time or a higher temperature is needed.
- **Iron on a firm, padded surface.** The padding helps absorb moisture from the pressing cloth.
- **Check the background.** Be sure the surface is clean and dry before you fuse.
- **Purchase matching or coordinating thread** for finishing the edges of your appliqués.
- **Keep a supply of hot iron cleaner** on hand. Available in most notion departments, the cleaner will remove any adhesive that may stick to your iron.

Traditions in Quilting

In The Pink

Shiloh's Courthouse Steps

The Round About Way

Danny's Quilt

Scrapbag Schoolhouse

Jane Anderson
Vinita, Oklahoma

Jane Anderson pieced her first quilt when she was only 10 years old. No one in her family quilted, nor did she know any quilters; but she had no doubt that she could do it! She made her patterns from newpapers, eyeballed the seams, and started sewing pieces together. One year later, she had a full-sized, hand-pieced quilt top. She didn't know what to do with it next, so she set it aside.

After experimenting with different kinds of needlework over the years, Jane returned to quilting in 1986. She is completely self-taught, never having taken a workshop or asking help from another quilter. "I taught myself by reading books, by trial and error, and by figuring out what works best for me," says Jane.

Joining the American Quilter's Society in 1989 and attending the show in Paducah changed her life. "It was a whole new world," she explains. "I was amazed, the quilts were so incredible! I started attending local shows and entering

"I taught myself by reading books, by trial and error, and by figuring out what works best for me"

my work whenever I could. Since retiring in 1999, I've been entering all the shows that I can. I love the competition! It challenges me to do my best and strive for improvement." Jane also joined two quilt guilds—the Grand Lake O' the Cherokee Quilt Guild in Grove, Oklahoma, and the Oklahoma State Quilter's Organization.

"I still have that first quilt top, pieced over 40 years ago," Jane recalls. "It's still not quilted and probably never will be. Some of the seams don't quite meet, and most of the blocks have holes in the center where the points meet. But all in all, I'm rather proud of it!"

In the Pink
2001

While examining her fabric collection one day, Jane noticed that she had several double pinks.

"I was wondering what I could do with them, since I don't especially like pink," says Jane. "But I remembered seeing an antique quilt with a color scheme I liked. It had double pink, mourning prints, and shirtings. I added purples and a few conversational prints

to my quilt and began piecing right away."

Jane is drawn to older, traditional quilt patterns. "Georgetown Circle is a block I haven't seen used very often," says Jane, "and I thought it would be perfect for a scrap quilt."

The pattern, though, is a challenging one. Jane completely hand-pieced and hand-quilted the

work. "I challenged myself to piece in the center circle, which would have been much easier to appliqué," Jane confesses.

But all of her hard work was not in vain. Jane finished the quilt just in time for the 2001 National Quilter's Association show, where it won second place in the Scrap Quilt category and received a special ribbon for Traditional Design.

In the Pink

Finished Size
Quilt: 79" x 99"
Blocks: 12 (20" x 20")

Materials
12 (18" x 22") fat quarters
    assorted pink prints for center
    star (A, B) and block back-
    ground (H)
12 (3" x 22") assorted strips
    light prints for Cs
12 (4" x 22") assorted strips
    light prints for Ds
12 (4" x 22") assorted strips dark
    prints for Ds
12 (5" x 22") assorted strips
    light prints for Es
12 (5" x 22") assorted strips pink
    or purple prints for Es
12 (9" x 22") assorted fat eighths
    dark prints for Fs
12 (9" x 22") assorted fat eighths
    light prints for Gs
¾ yards black print for inner border
3¼ yards pink print for outer
    border and binding
6 yards backing fabric
Queen-size batting

Cutting
Each strip is 1 set. Patterns are
on pages 64–65. **Cut pieces in
order listed to make best use
of yardage.**
From each pink print, cut:
- 4 Hs.
- 1 A.
- 8 Bs.
From each light print (C), cut:
- 8 Cs.
From each light print (D), cut:
- 8 Ds.
From each dark print (D), cut:
- 8Ds.

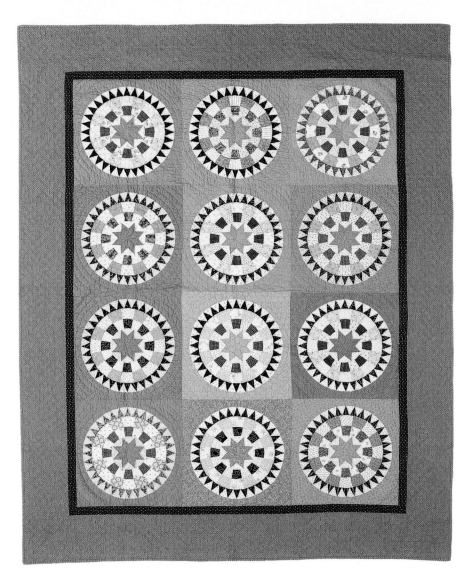

From each light print (E), cut:
- 8 Es.
*From each pink or purple print
(E), cut:*
- 8 Es.
From each dark print (F), cut:
- 32 Fs.
From each light print (G), cut:
- 32 Gs.
From black print, cut:
- 9 (2" x 42") strips. Piece
  strips to make 2 (2" x 80")
  inner top and bottom borders
  and 2 (2" x 100") inner side
  borders.
From pink print, cut:
- 9 (8½" x 42") strips. Piece

strips to make 2 (2" x 80")
outer top and bottom borders
and 2 (2" x 100") outer side
borders.
- 10 (2¼" x 42") strips for
  binding.

Block Assembly
Refer to *Block Assembly Diagram*
throughout.
1. Choose 1 set each pink
A/B/H, light C, light D, dark
D, light E, pink or purple E,
dark F, and light G.
2. Join 1 B to 1 C to make 1 unit,
matching dots. Make 8 units.
Join units into pairs, then pair

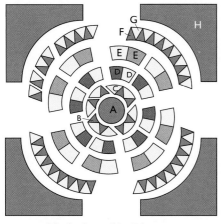

Block Assembly Diagram

again until ring is formed. Press. Piece or appliqué A in center.

3. Join 1 dark and 1 light D to make 1 unit. Make 8 units. Join in pairs as above to make D ring. Press. Piece or appliqué A/B/C circle to D ring, centering star points on light Ds.

4. Join 1 purple and 1 light E to make 1 unit. Make 8 units. Join in pairs as above to make E ring. Press. Piece or appliqué D circle to E ring, matching seams and purple Es to light Ds.

5. Join 1 dark F and 1 light G to make 1 unit, matching dots. Make 32 units. Join in pairs as above to make 1 F/G ring. Piece or appliqué E circle to F/G ring. Triangle bases should be centered on each E piece.

6. Join 4 Hs on short legs to

make block background. Piece or appliqué circle to background, orienting pink star as shown, and matching F points with H seams.

7. Make 12 Georgetown blocks (*Block Diagram*).

Quilt Assembly

1. Referring to *Quilt Top Assembly Diagram,* lay out blocks in 4 horizontal rows of 3 blocks each. Join into rows; join rows to complete quilt center.

2. Join 1 black inner border to 1 pink outer border, matching lengths, to make 1 border strip. Make 4 border strips. Center border strips on each side of quilt and join. Miter corners.

Quilting and Finishing

1. Divide backing fabric into 2 (3-yard) lengths. Cut 1 piece in half lengthwise. Sew 1 narrow panel to each side of wide panel. Press seam allowances toward narrow panels.

2. Layer backing, batting, and quilt top; baste. Quilt as desired. Quilt shown is outline-quilted in triangles, forming a zigzag ring. D and E rings are quilted in circles. Backgrounds are quilted in concentric circles, forming diamonds at block intersections. Outer border is quilted in double diamonds.

3. Join 2¼"-wide pink print strips into 1 continuous piece for straight-grain French-fold binding. Add binding to quilt.

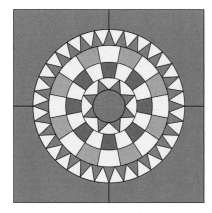

Block Diagram

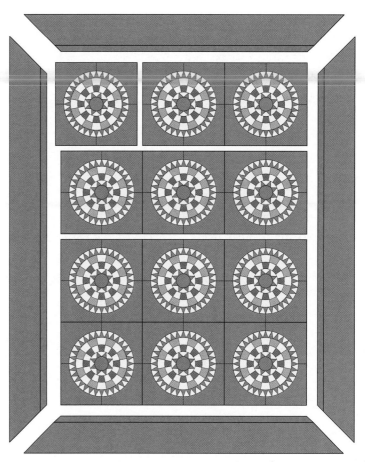

Quilt Top Assembly Diagram

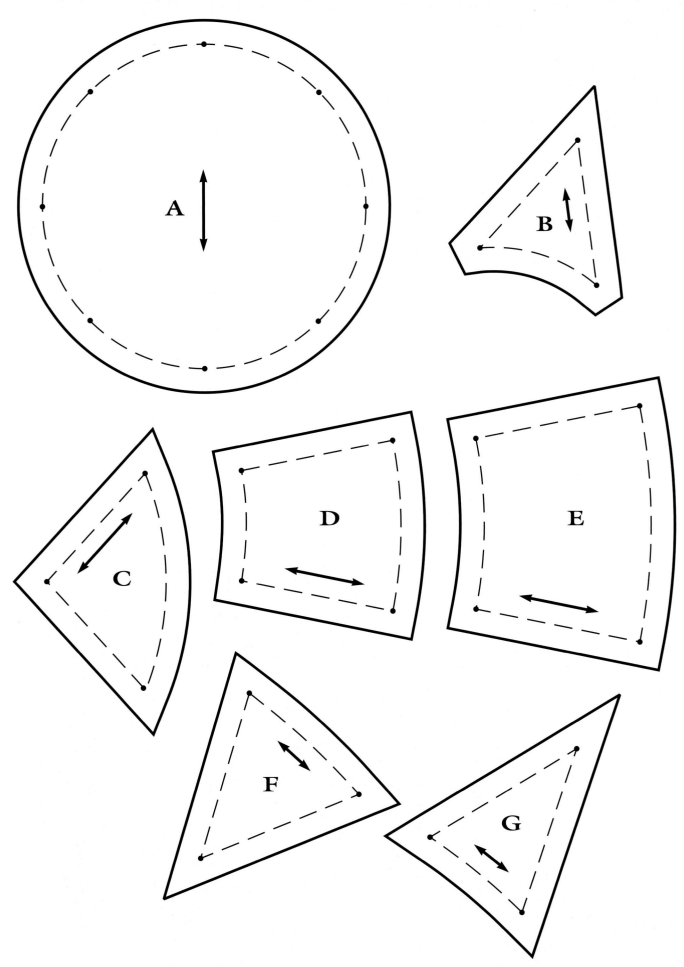

A

B

C

D

E

F

G

64

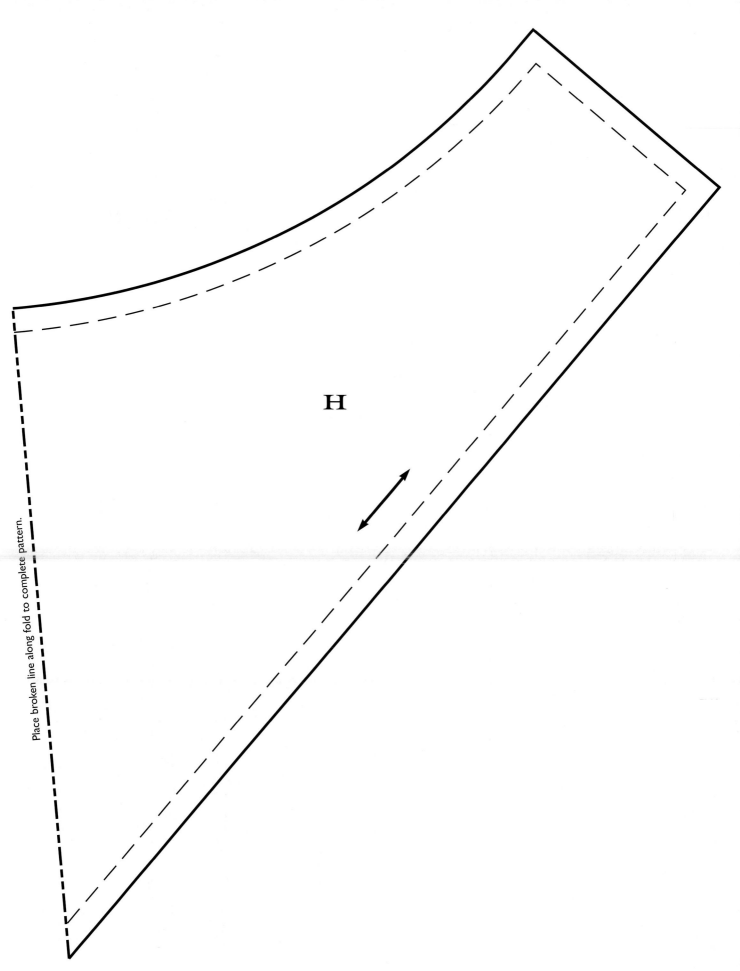

H

Place broken line along fold to complete pattern.

65

Elaine McGarry
Fayetteville, Tennessee

Elaine McGarry learned to sew in her junior high home economics class. When her children were small, she developed an interest in quilting. But at the time, she was a dedicated smocker. "I decided to postpone my quilting desires until my children would no longer wear smocked clothing, so I could devote my full attention to quilting," says Elaine. "I took my first class in 1981, but my obsession with quilting really took off in 1993."

Now Elaine is an active member of two quilting groups: The Fussy Cutters quilting bee in her hometown, and the Heritage Quilters of Huntsville, a guild in Huntsville, Alabama, not far from the Alabama/Tennessee state line.

"If I don't get to quilt every day, I begin to get cranky."

"If I don't get to quilt every day, I begin to get cranky," Elaine says. "My family tells me I am obsessed, which I do not see as a negative comment. I usually have 10 quilts in progress at all times. I work on the one that calls out the loudest."

Elaine focuses her work on antique patterns and reproduction fabrics reminiscent of the late 1800s. She machine-pieces her quilt tops, but prefers to hand-quilt the finished product.

Elaine sums up her work best when she says, "As all quilters, my quilts are very personal to me and are made with heart and soul."

Shiloh's Courthouse Steps
2002

Elaine McGarry intended her traditional Courthouse Steps quilt to be a wall hanging for a class she was going to teach. However, she had so much fun making the blocks, she couldn't resist making more and more!

"I enjoy working with reproduction fabrics," says Elaine, "Since I have no old family quilts of my own, I have to make my own family heirlooms. My interest in history has drawn me to Civil War era quilts, which is the time frame I strive to replicate."

In April 2001, after attending a re-enactment of the Battle of Shiloh, Tennessee, Elaine knew what she would title her quilt. *Shiloh's Courthouse Steps* was the result.

Shiloh's Courthouse Steps

Finished Size
Quilt: 74" x 89¾"
Blocks: 104 (7½" x 6¾")
  Courthouse Steps Blocks
18 (6" x 6") Sawtooth Star Blocks
8 (6" x 6") LeMoyne Star Blocks

Materials
Note: All fabrics are Civil War Reproduction prints.
12–15 fat quarters (18" x 22") assorted light prints for blocks
18–22 fat quarters (18" x 22") assorted dark prints for blocks
1 fat quarter (18" x 22") purple print for block centers
¾ yard light stripe for sashing and borders
¾ yard dark print for binding
5½ yards backing fabric
Full-size batting

Cutting
Instructions are for rotary cutting and quick piecing. Border strips are exact length needed. You may want to cut them longer to allow for piecing variations.
From light prints, cut:
- 104 light Courthouse Steps block sets of:
  - 2 (1¼" x 1¼") squares.
  - 2 (1¼" x 2¾") strips.
  - 2 (1¼" x 4¼") strips.
  - 2 (1¼" x 5¾") strips.
  - Divide into 2 sets of 1 strip each.
- 8 Eight Point Star background sets of:
  - 1 (3¾" x 3¾") square. Cut square in quarters diagonally to make 4 B triangles.
  - 4 (2¼" x 2¼") C squares.
- 18 Sawtooth Star background

sets of:
  - 4 (2" x 3½") D rectangles.
  - 4 (2" x 2") G squares.
From dark prints, cut:
- 104 dark Courthouse Steps block sets of:
  - 2 (1¼" x 3½") strips.
  - 2 (1¼" x 5") strips.
  - 2 (1¼" x 6½") strips.
  - 2 (1¼" x 8") strips.
  - Divide into 2 sets of 1 strip each.
- 8 LeMoyne Star sets of:
  - 2 (1¾" x 22") strips. Cut strips into 8 (1¾") A diamonds using 45° markings on ruler *(Cutting Diagram)*, or use template A on page 69.

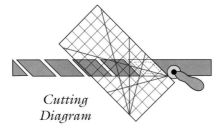
Cutting Diagram

- 18 Sawtooth Star sets of:
  - 1 (3½" x 3½") F square.
  - 8 (2" x 2") E squares.
From purple print, cut:
- 10 (1¼" x 22") strips. Cut strips into 104 (1¼" x 2") strips for block centers.
From light stripe for sashing and borders, cut:
- 5 (1¼" x 42") strips. Cut strips into 26 (1¼" x 6½") sashing strips.
- 9 (1½" x 42") strips. Piece strips to make 1 (1½" x 60½") bottom border, 2 (1½" x 89¼") side borders, and 1 (1½" x 74½") top border. Cut 2 (1½" x 6½") bottom sashing strips for pieced side borders from remainder.
From dark print, cut:
- 9 (2¼" x 42") strips for binding.

Courthouse Steps Block Assembly
1. Choose 1 purple strip and 2 sets each light and dark fabrics. Also choose matching set for 1 each light and dark fabrics.
2. Begin working in upper left corner. Lay out 4 sets as shown in *Courthouse Steps Block Diagram.*

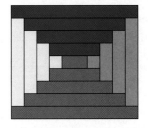
Courthouse Steps Block Diagram

Place second set of light #2 to right of block; place second set of dark #2 below block *(Fabric Arrangement Diagram)*. These will be used in adjoining blocks.

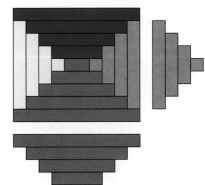
Fabric Arrangement Diagram

3. Place 1¼" x 1¼" square from light #1 atop left end of purple strip, right sides facing. Stitch and open out. Repeat with light #2 on right end to complete center strip *(Courthouse Steps Assembly Diagram 1)*.

Courthouse Steps Block Assembly Diagram 1

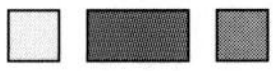

4. Join 1¼" x 3½" dark #1 strip to top of center strip. Repeat with dark #2 on bottom of center strip (*Courthouse Steps Assembly Diagram 2*).

Courthouse Steps Block Assembly Diagram 2

5. Add matching light side pieces and then top and bottom for next round (*Courthouse Steps Assembly Diagram 3*).

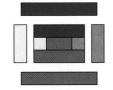

Courthouse Steps Block Assembly Diagram 3

6. Add matching light side pieces and then top and bottom for next round (*Courthouse Steps Assembly Diagram 4*).

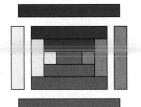

Courthouse Steps Block Assembly Diagram 4

7. Add final matching pieces to complete block (*Courthouse Steps Assembly Diagram 5*).

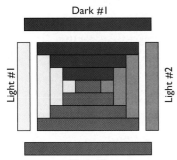

Courthouse Steps Block Assembly Diagram 5

8. The matching light set becomes light #1 for second block. Choose 2 matching sets of light fabrics for light #2 and place second set to right of second block. Choose 2 dark sets plus matching set for 1 dark; place as before. Repeat block assembly for second block. (See quilt photo or *Quilt Top Assembly Diagram*.)

9. Continue block assembly to make top row of 8 blocks. Begin second row, using dark set reserved from first block.

10. Make 13 rows of 8 blocks each. Odd sets of lights and darks should be used for edge fabrics.

LeMoyne Star Assembly

1. Referring to *LeMoyne Star Block Assembly Diagram 1*, join 8 A diamonds in pairs. Join pairs as shown to make star.

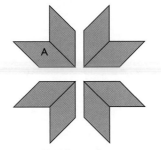

LeMoyne Star Block Assembly Diagram 1

2. Referring to *LeMoyne Star Block Assembly Diagram 2*, set in B triangles.

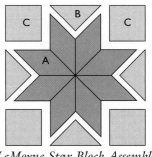

LeMoyne Star Block Assembly Diagram 2

3. Set in C squares to complete 1 LeMoyne Star (*LeMoyne Star Block Diagram*). Make 8 LeMoyne Stars.

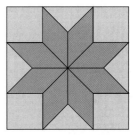

LeMoyne Star Block Diagram

Sawtooth Star Assembly

1. Referring to *Diagonal Seams Diagram*, place 1 E square atop 1 end of 1 D rectangle. Stitch diagonally from corner to corner as shown. Trim excess fabric ¼" from stitching. Press open to reveal triangle. Repeat on opposite end to make 1 Goose Chase unit. Make 4 Goose Chase units.

Diagonal Seams Diagram

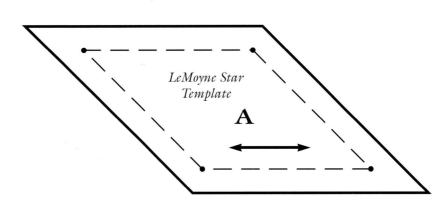

LeMoyne Star Template

A

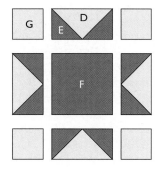

Sawtooth Star
Block Assembly Diagram

2. Referring to *Sawtooth Star Block Assembly Diagram*, lay out 4 Goose Chase units, 1 F square, and 4 G squares. Join into rows; join rows to complete 1 Sawtooth Star *(Sawtooth Star Block Diagram)*. Make 18 Sawtooth Stars.

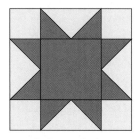

Sawtooth Star Block Diagram

Quilt Assembly

Refer to *Quilt Top Assembly Diagram* throughout.

1. Blocks should be laid out in rows from assembly. Join blocks into rows; join rows to complete quilt center.

2. Join light stripe bottom border to quilt.

3. Join light stripe side borders to quilt.

4. Alternate 4 LeMoyne Stars and 9 Sawtooth Stars with 13 (1¼" x 6½") sashing strips as shown, placing stars as desired. Place 1 (1½" x 6½") sashing strip at

bottom. Join to make 1 side border. Repeat for second side border. Add to quilt.

5. Add light stripe top border to quilt.

Quilting and Finishing

1. Divide backing fabric into 2 (2¾-yard) lengths. Cut 1 piece in half lengthwise. Sew 1 narrow panel to each side of wide panel. Press seam allowances toward narrow panels.

2. Layer backing, batting, and quilt top; baste. Quilt as desired. Quilt shown is quilted in clamshells. Star blocks are quilted in-the-ditch around blocks, with outline quilting in background and a star in each center.

3. Join 2¼"-wide dark strips into 1 continuous piece for straight-grain French-fold binding. Add binding to quilt.

Quilt Top Assembly Diagram

Leslie Rego
Sun Valley, Idaho

*L*eslie Rego began quilting in 1982 when she was pregnant with her first child and living in Guatemala. She only had one quilting book, and she chose the pattern with the most templates. "Of course, I quickly got bogged down, and it took a long time to finish the piece," says Leslie. "I call it *Big Quilt!*"

Leslie finished her second quilt the day before her daughter was born. It was a simple piece, with two colors against a muslin background. "The whole process was incredibly boring," Leslie recalls. So when she became pregnant with her second child, she decided she had to do something more creative. While on a business trip to Miami from Guatemala, she visited a quilt shop and bought 30 ¼-yard pieces of different peach and orange fabrics. "I arrived home and happily pieced 30 different squares for my second baby quilt," Leslie says. "For the first time, I enjoyed the quiltmaking process."

"It has taken me a long time to free myself artistically...."

In 1993, Leslie entered a quilt she made for her third child, Delamon, titled *Delamon's Comet.* She was thrilled when it was juried into the American Quilter's Society show in Paducah, Kentucky, and won third place in the theme category. Since then, her works have been in national shows, and two have been published.

"I easily use 50 or more fabrics—sometimes over 100—in a piece," Leslie says. "I especially love to include Indonesian batiks and hand-woven fabric from Guatemala into my quilts. I like to work with unlikely color combinations and asymmetrical designs."

The Round About Way
2000

The quilt's name, *The Round About Way,* has two meanings for Leslie Rego.

"One meaning reflects the pattern of the quilt, all the circles and paths leading in and out, meandering across the quilt face," says Leslie. "The title also reflects my journey as a quilter," Leslie shares. "It has taken me a long time to free myself artistically and I have not always taken a straight path. In fact, it has been the round about journeys that have added up to my artistic expression today."

The Round About Way

Finished Size

Quilt: 58½" x 70½"
Blocks: 80 (6" x 6")

Materials

20 to 25 fat quarters (18" x 22")
  assorted batiks and prints for
  blocks
½ yard light border fabric
½ yard medium border fabric
¾ yard dark border fabric
1 yard fabric for binding
4 yards backing fabric
Twin-size batting
Metallic thread for embroidery

Cutting

Patterns are on page 74. **Cut
pieces in order listed to make
best use of yardage.**

From assorted batiks and prints, cut:
• 80 As.
• 80 Bs.

From light border fabric, cut:
• 7 (1½" x 42") strips. Piece
  to make 2 (1½" x 60") top
  and bottom borders and
  2 (1½" x 72") side borders.

From medium border fabric, cut:
• 7 (2¼" x 42") strips. Piece
  to make 2 (2¼" x 60") top
  and bottom borders and
  2 (2¼" x 72") side borders.

From dark border fabric, cut:
• 7 (3" x 42") strips. Piece to
  make 2 (3" x 60") top and
  bottom borders and 2 (3" x 72")
  side borders.

From binding fabric, cut:
• 1 (30" x 30") square for binding.

Block Assembly

Refer to *Block Assembly Diagram*.

1. Choose 1 A
and 1 B. Blocks
can coordinate or
contrast as
desired; see photo
for color combi-
nations used in
original quilt.

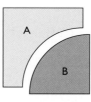

*Block Assembly
Diagram*

2. Fold each piece in half and
finger-press to make a small crease
along outer curved edge to mark
the center of curve.

3. With right sides facing and A
on top, match center creases and
ends and pin. Stitch along curved
edges, aligning and smoothing as
you go. Clip seams and press

seam allowances
toward B.

4. Make 80 blocks
(Block Diagram).

Block Diagram

Quilt Assembly

1. Referring to *Quilt Top Assembly
Diagram,* lay out blocks in 10 horizontal rows of 8 blocks each.
Rotate blocks as shown or as
desired. When satisfied with placement, join into rows; join rows to
complete quilt center.

2. Machine-embroider vines
around curves of blocks as shown
in photo, or as desired with metallic embroidery thread.

3. Join 60"-long borders in order:
light, medium, dark. Make 2 top

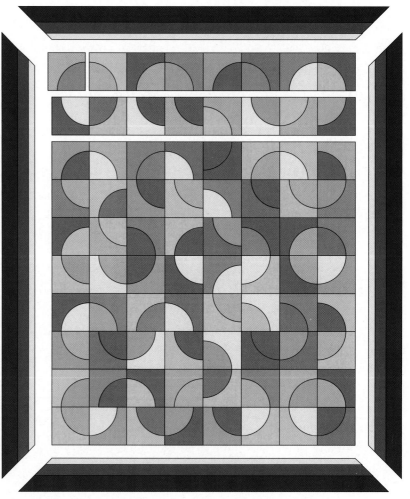

Quilt Top Assembly Diagram

and bottom border strips. Repeat with 72"-long strips for side border strips.

4. Center border strips on each side of quilt and join. Miter corners. Use a dinner plate to draw guidelines for rounding corners, if desired.

Quilting and Finishing

1. Divide backing fabric into 2 (2-yard) lengths. Cut 1 piece in half lengthwise. Sew 1 narrow panel to each side of wide panel. Press seam allowances toward narrow panels. Seams will run horizontally.

2. Layer backing, batting, and quilt top; baste. Quilt as desired. Quilt shown is closely meander-quilted.

3. Make 8 yards of 2¼"-wide bias binding from binding fabric square. Add binding to quilt. Trim corners before stitching binding to back of quilt.

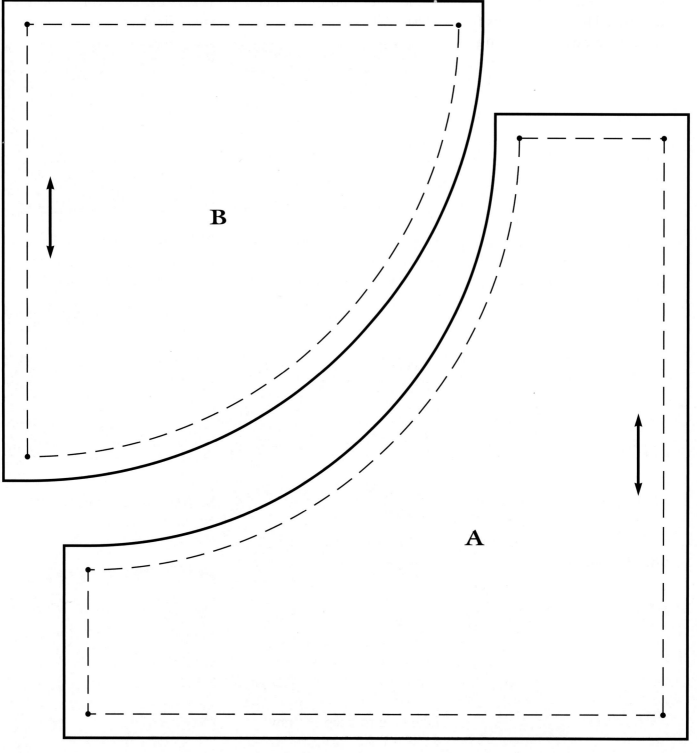

PIECING CURVES

Some quilters believe that curved seams are best sewn by hand, while others prefer to use the machine. With a little practice, you can sew curved seams quickly on the sewing machine.

As a general rule, the larger the curved seam, the easier it will be to sew it on the machine. The main secrets for success are carefully pinning and gently tugging the fabric as you sew. We suggest using fine silk pins for pinning, because they are very thin and will reduce buckling in your block.

1. After you've cut out the block pieces, fold each one in half and make a finger crease to find the center. With right sides facing, pin at the center match points *(Photo A)*.

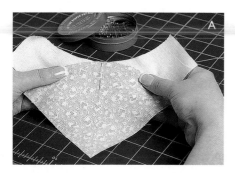

2. Next, align the raw edges of your inner and outer curved pieces along the left side and pin *(Photo B)*.

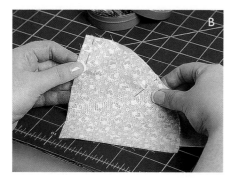

3. Aligning the curved edges, pin the loose area between the left side and the center *(Photo C)*.

4. Repeat Steps 2 and 3 for the right side of the curve. When you're done, the unit should look like *Photo D*. The block will look buckled.

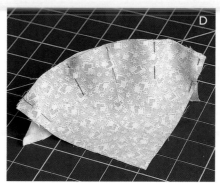

5. It is crucial to have a ¼" seam guide on your sewing machine to keep your seam even. Sew slowly. Every few stitches, pause to turn the unit and give the bottom piece a little tug. That will prevent puckers and tucks as you sew. However, you must take care to keep the raw edges of the curves aligned.

6. Remove the pins. Clip along the curved seam allowance *(Photo E)*. This will make the curve lie flat.

7. Using a steam iron, press the seam allowance toward the darker fabric *(Photo F)*.

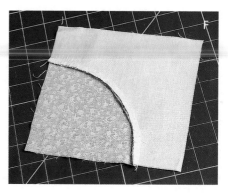

8. You should have a beautiful curve with no tucks or puckers *(Photo G)*.

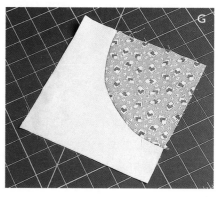

Ruth Ann Johnson
Whittier, California

*uth Ann Johnson received her first quilt when she was born. It was a doll quilt made by her great-grandmother, who was 94 at the time. However, it was Ruth Ann's sister, Patricia Nicoll, who introduced her to quilting years later in 1989. (Patricia's work, *Diana's Rose,* appeared in *Great American Quilts 2002.*)

"I [put] a lot of myself into the quilt."

"Pat sent me a book on how to hand quilt, along with some needles and a thimble," Ruth Ann recalls. "I remember practicing the stitch and thinking, 'This is so hard! But if Pat can do it, so can I!'"

In 1990, Ruth Ann took a beginning quilt sampler class at a local quilt shop to learn the basics. She made two Log Cabin quilts—one for her son David and one for her daughter Christina.

When she joined the Friendship Square Quilt Guild and the Small Threads of Friendship group in 1994, Ruth Ann stretched herself even further. "I was inspired by the wonderful quilts the speakers shared and I was impressed with the talented ladies in the guild," Ruth Ann says. "I made many new friends in the guild."

Now Ruth Ann and Pat enjoy many hours together quilting. "We have shopped for fabric, gone to quilt shows, shared ideas, encouraged each other, and rejoiced in each other's accomplishments," says Ruth Ann. She enjoys making quilts as gifts for family and friends and enters her quilts in state and local fairs.

Danny's Quilt
2001

When Ruth Ann's friend Danny shared his joy of sailing with her, she shared her love of quilting with him.

"I realized that he has a great appreciation for other people's handwork, and I knew I wanted to make him a quilt," says Ruth Ann. "When I shared my intentions with him, Danny said he felt honored and humbled. He knew it would be a lot of hard work and that I would be putting a lot of myself into the quilt."

Ruth Ann wanted to make the quilt in colors that Danny would enjoy, so she took him to The Calico House quilt shop in Yorba Linda, California, to pick out the colors.

"He was very interested in the quilting process, so I shared each stage of the project with him," says Ruth Ann.

She chose the traditional Goose in the Pond block and designed the outer borders with Flying Geese units. The stunning combination won her a first-place ribbon at the Los Angeles County Fair in Pomona, Caifornia.

"Danny really loved having the quilt named after him," Ruth Ann shares. "But I asked him if he had to come up with a name for the quilt, what would it be? He responded *'Midnight Storm at Sea,'* which I think describes his quilt perfectly."

Danny's Quilt

Finished Size

Quilt: 84½" x 101"
Blocks: 20 (15" x 15")

Materials

7½ yards solid black for blocks, sashing, borders, and binding
20 fat quarters (18" x 22") assorted green, blue, and purple batiks for blocks
⅜ yard light green batik for inner border
1 yard purple batik for borders
1½ yards dark blue, green, and purple batik for pieced border
7½ yards backing fabric
Queen-size batting

Cutting

Instructions are for rotary cutting and quick piecing. Border strips are exact length needed. You may want to cut them longer to allow for piecing variations. **Cut pieces in order listed to make best use of yardage.**

From black, cut:

- 30 (1½" x 42") strips. Cut strips in half to make 60 (1½" x 22") strips for strip sets.
- 10 (3½" x 42") strips. Cut strips into 100 (3½") squares for blocks and 8 (3½") squares for border corners.
- 12 (3⅞" x 42") strips. Cut strips into 120 (3⅞") squares for half-square triangles.
- 25 (2" x 42") strips. Cut strips into 49 (2" x 15½") sashing strips and 30 (2") sashing squares.
- 10 (2½" x 42") strips. Piece to make 2 (2½" x 97½") side borders and 2 (2½" x 85") top and bottom borders.

- 8 (2½" x 42") strips. Cut strips into 64 (2½" x 4½") border rectangles.
- 10 (2¼" x 42") strips for binding.

From each fat quarter of batiks, cut:

- 3 (1½" x 22") strips for strip sets. Cut 1 strip into 4 (1½") squares for block corners; reserve remainder for Strip Set A.
- 2 (3⅞" x 22") strips. Cut strips into 6 (3⅞") squares for half-square triangles.

From light green batik, cut:

- 6 (1½" x 42") strips. Piece strips to make 2 (1½" x 84½") inner side borders and 2 (1½" x 70") inner top and bottom borders.

From purple batik, cut:

- 18 (1¼" x 42") strips. Piece strips to make 2 (1¼" x 86½") inner side borders, 2 (1¼" x 71½") inner top and bottom borders, 2 (1¼" x 96") outer side borders, and 2 (1¼" x 81") outer top and bottom borders.

From dark batik, cut:

- 6 (4½" x 42") strips. Cut strips into 4 (4½" x 20") top and bottom border pieces, 4 (4½" x 28¼") side border pieces, and 4 (4½") squares for border corners.
- 8 (2½" x 42") strips. Cut strips into 128 (2½") squares for border units.

Block Assembly

1. Join 2 black and 1 batik strip to make 1 Strip Set A. (Use short batik strip for Set A.) Cut strip set into 8 (1½"-wide) A segments.

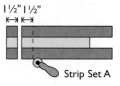
Strip Set A

2. Join 2 batik and 1 black strip to make 1 Strip Set B. Cut strip set into 4 (1½"-wide) B segments and 4 (3½"-wide) side units for block center.

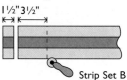
Strip Set B

3. Referring to *Nine-Patch Assembly Diagram*, lay out 2 A and 1 B segments. Join to make 1 Nine-Patch unit.

A B A
Nine-Patch and Side Unit Assembly Diagram

Make 4 Nine-Patch units.

4. Referring to *Center Assembly Diagram*, lay out 4 Nine-Patch units, 4 side units, and 1 black square. Join into rows; join rows to complete block center.

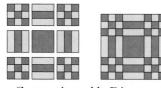

Center Assembly Diagram

5. Referring to *Half-Square Triangle Assembly Diagram*, draw a diagonal line from corner to corner on back of batik 3⅞" squares. Place 1 batik and 1 black square together, right sides facing. Stitch ¼" from line on both sides. Cut apart and press open to make 2 half-square triangle units. Make 12 units.

Half-Square Triangle Assembly Diagram

6. Referring to *Block Corner Assembly Diagram*, place 1 batik 1½"

Block Corner Assembly Diagram

square on black corner of 1 half-square triangle unit. Using diagonal seams, stitch diagonally across square. Trim ¼" from stitching and press open to make 1 block corner unit. Make 4 block corner units.

7. Referring to *Block Assembly Diagram*, lay out center, 8 half-square triangle units, 4 black squares, and 4 block corner units. Join into sections as shown; add to center to complete 1 block (*Block Diagram*).

8. Make 20 blocks.

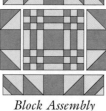

Block Assembly Diagram

Block Diagram

Quilt Assembly

Refer to *Quilt Top Assembly Diagram* throughout.

1. Lay out blocks, sashing, and sashing squares. Join into rows; join rows to complete quilt center.

2. Add green inner side borders to quilt. Add top and bottom borders.

3. Add purple inner side borders to quilt. Add top and bottom borders.

Diagonal Seams Diagram

4. Referring to *Diagonal Seams Diagram*, place 1 batik 2½" square atop 1 end of 1 black 2½" x 4½" rectangle. Stitch diagonally from corner to corner. Trim excess fabric ¼" from stitching. Press open to reveal triangle. Repeat on opposite end to complete 1 goose chase border unit. Make 64 border units.

5. Referring to *Border Corner Assembly Diagram*, place 1 black 3½"

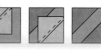

Border Corner Assembly Diagram

square atop 1 corner of 1 (4½") batik square. Using diagonal seams, stitch, trim, and press open to reveal triangle. Repeat on opposite corner to make 1 border corner unit. Make 4 border corner units.

6. Join 6 border units to make 1 middle border segment. Make 4 middle border segments.

7. Join 5 border units to make 1 corner segment. Make 8 corner segments.

8. Join 1 middle border segment, 2 corner segments, and 2 (4½" x 28¼") border pieces to make 1 side border. Repeat for second side border. Add to quilt.

9. Join 2 border corner units, 2 corner segments, 1 middle segment, and 2 (4½" x 20") border pieces to make top border. Repeat for bottom border. Add to quilt.

10. Add outer purple side borders to quilt. Add top and bottom borders.

11. Add black side borders to quilt. Add top and bottom borders.

Quilting and Finishing

1. Divide backing fabric into 3 (2½-yard) lengths. Join along sides to make backing. Seams will run horizontally.

2. Layer backing, batting, and quilt top; baste. Quilt as desired. Quilt shown is quilted in-the-ditch.

3. Join 2¼"-wide black strips into 1 continuous piece for straight-grain French-fold binding. Add binding to quilt.

Quilt Top Assembly Diagram

Judie Rothermel
Canton, Ohio

*J*udie Rothermel and her husband Bob owned and operated the Schoolhouse Quilt Shoppe in Canton, Ohio, from 1976–2001. Now, Judie focuses her attention full-time on designing fabrics, writing books, and promoting the Schoolhouse Web site.

Through a collaborative effort with Marcus Brothers Textiles, Inc., Judie has designed numerous reproduction fabrics for the quilt market. For the last 15 years, she has produced at least eight fabric lines per year. You may own pieces from her collections such as Discover America, Baltimore Album Prints, Civil War Prints, Emily's Calico Garden, Miniature Collectibles, and the popular Aunt Grace series.

> *"I use my personal collection of antique textiles as a guide."*

"I use my personal collection of antique textiles as a guide," Judie explains. "I design each fabric line to coordinate with previous lines."

In addition to designing fabrics, Judie has written several books—one on miniatures, and several on patchwork—featuring quilts made from her fabrics.

Scrapbag Schoolhouse
1986

Scrapbag Schoolhouse launched Judie Rothermel's career as a fabric designer for Marcus Brothers Textiles. The Schoolhouse block is a long-time favorite pattern of Judie's. She made the quilt to display in her store, Schoolhouse Quilt Shoppe.

The quilt caught the attention of a Marcus Brothers salesman who came to the shop to take Judie's order for fabric. The salesman returned to his home office and told his colleages of Judie's talents. This led to her meeting Marcus Brothers executives in 1987 and to her career as a professional fabric designer. To learn more, visit her Web site at: www.schoolhousequilts.com

Scrapbag Schoolhouse

Finished Size
Quilt: 77" x 94½"
Blocks: 30 (10" x 10¾")

Materials
30 fat eighths (9" x 22") assorted
    prints for schoolhouses
5 yards muslin for block back-
    ground, sashing, and borders
2½ yards brown print for borders
    and binding
5½ yards backing fabric
Full-size batting

Cutting
Instructions are for rotary cutting
and quick piecing. Border strips
are exact length needed. You may
want to make them longer to
allow for piecing variations.
Patterns are on pages 84–85.
**Cut pieces in order listed to
make best use of yardage.**

From each print, cut:
- 1 (1¾" x 22") strip. Cut strip
  into 2 (1¾" x 3½") G rectangles,
  1 (1¾" x 4½") I rectangle, and
  2 (1¾" x 5") N rectangles.
- 1 (2" x 22") strip. Cut strip
  into 2 (2" x 2¼") B rectangles,
  2 (¾" x 1⅜") K rectangles,
  1 (1½" x 3") L rectangle, and
  2 (1⅜" x 3") M rectangles.
- 1 D.
- 1 F.

From muslin, cut:
- 2¼ yards. Cut yardage into
  4 (3½" x 81") lengthwise strips.
  Cut strips into 25 (3½" x 10½")
  horizontal sashing strips.
- Cut yardage into 4 (3½" x 81")
  lengthwise strips. Trim to make 4
  (3½" x 80") vertical sashing strips.

- Cut yardage into 4 (2½" x 81")
  lengthwise strips. Cut strips into
  2 (2½" x 80") side borders and
  2 (2½" x 66½") top and bottom
  borders.
- 3 (4¼" x 42") strips. Cut strips
  into 26 (4¼") squares. Cut
  squares in quarters diagonally to
  make 104 triangles for pieced
  borders.
- 3 (2¼" x 42") strips. Cut strips
  into 30 (2¼" x 3½") A rectangles.
- 30 Cs.
- 30 Cs reversed.
- 30 Es.
- 13 (2" x 42") strips. Cut strips
  into 30 (2" x 3½") H rectangles,
  30 (2" x 5½") O rectangles,

and 30 (2" x 6½") P rectangles.
- 5 (1⅜" x 42") strips. Cut
  strips into 120 (1⅜" x 1⅝") J
  rectangles.

From brown print, cut:
- 4 (4½" x 90") lengthwise
  strips. Trim strips to make
  2 (4½" x 87") side borders and
  2 (4½" x 77½") top and
  bottom borders.
- 5 (2¼" x 90") lengthwise strips
  for binding.
- 2 (4¼" x 90") lengthwise strips.
  Cut strips into 25 (4¼")
  squares. Cut squares in quarters
  diagonally to make 100 triangles
  for pieced borders.

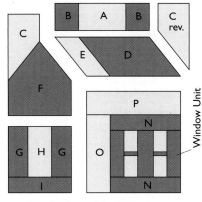

Block Assembly Diagram

Block Assembly

Refer to *Block Assembly Diagram* throughout.

1. Join 1 print B to opposite ends of 1 A to make chimney unit.

2. Join 1 E to 1 D for roof. Add chimney unit to roof. Set in 1 C rev. for corner.

3. Referring to *Window Unit Assembly Diagram*, join 1 J to each long side of 1 K to make window unit. Repeat. Join window units with 1 L. Add 1 M to outside edges of unit. Add 1 N to top and bottom. Add 1 O to left side. Add 1 P to top to complete house front. Join to roof unit.

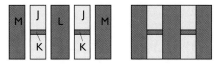

Window Unit Assembly Diagram

4. Join 1 G to each long side of 1 H. Add 1 I to bottom for door unit. Add 1 F to top. Join to house front. Set in 1 C to complete 1 Schoolhouse block *(Block Diagram)*.

5. Make 30 Schoolhouse blocks.

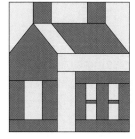

Block Diagram

Quilt Assembly

Refer to *Quilt Top Assembly Diagram* throughout.

1. Lay out 6 blocks and 5 sashing strips in a vertical row as shown. Join to make 1 row. Make 5 vertical rows.

2. Alternate 5 vertical rows and 4 sashing strips. Join to complete quilt center.

3. Add muslin side borders to quilt. Add top and bottom borders.

4. Join 22 print and 23 muslin triangles to make top border. Repeat for bottom border.

5. Join 28 print and 29 muslin triangles to make 1 side border. Repeat for second border. *(Note: Instructions call for 1 less triangle than in quilt shown for mathematical ease.)*

6. Join borders to quilt, matching seams at corners.

7. Add print side borders to quilt. Add top and bottom borders.

Quilting and Finishing

1. Divide backing fabric into 2 (2¾-yard) lengths. Cut 1 piece in half lengthwise. Sew 1 narrow panel to each side of wide panel. Press seam allowances toward narrow panels.

2. Layer backing, batting, and quilt top; baste. Quilt as desired. Quilt shown is outline-quilted in blocks. Sashing and borders are filled with diagonal grid.

3. Join 2¼"-wide print strips into 1 continuous piece for straight-grain French-fold binding. Add binding to quilt.

Quilt Top Assembly Diagram

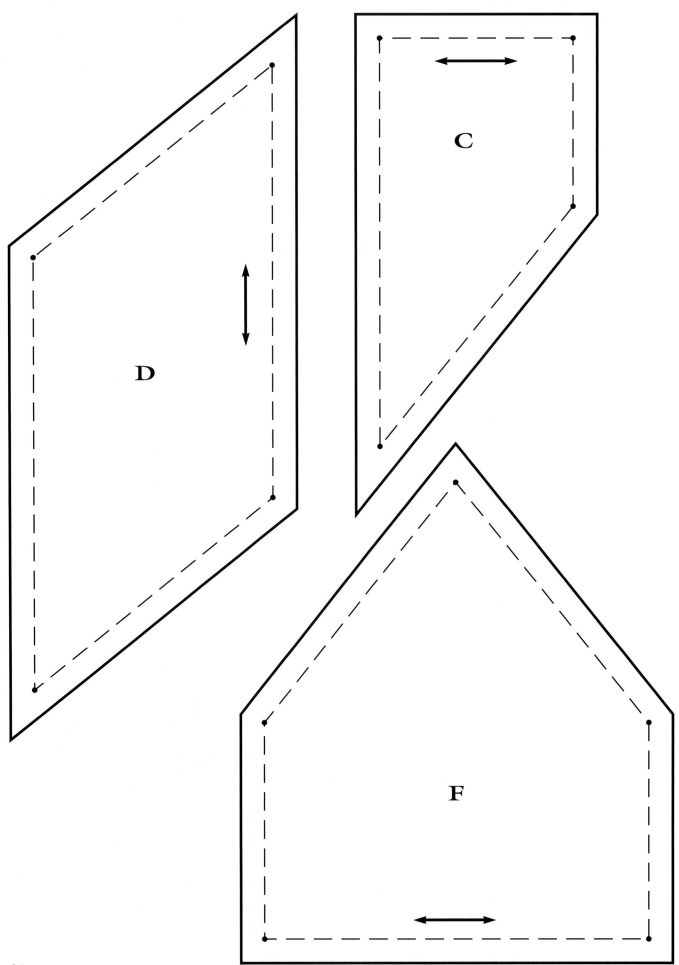

D

C

F

E

Trace, scan, or photocopy this quilt label to finish your quilt.

Bee Quilters

Out-of-Towners
Oak Ridge, Tennessee

Candace Tucker, Tone Haugen-Cogburn, Patty Ashworth, and Bridget Matlock (shown left to right in adjacent photo) make up the Out-of-Towners. The four met through the Smoky Mountain Quilt Guild about seven years ago, and formed their own small group three years later.

"We all wanted feedback on original projects that we were doing for contests and shows," says Patty Ashworth. "Then we decided it would be fun to make one quilt as a group. We decided up front that none of us 'owned' the quilt. This way, we hoped to avoid any disagreements."

"We don't do rules, and we love to laugh!"

There is no leader of this group. "We don't do rules, and we love to laugh!" says Patty. Each member has an equal say on each step of the quilting process. Since each person has her own strong points, the workload is distributed equally.

"Quilting is a major part of our lives, and our families understand this," says Patty. "We have given up as much housework as possible to find time to quilt! Even with just four friends, it's difficult to match our busy schedules and find times when we can all get together. But each one of us quilts every day."

Sunday Quilt
2000

The Out-of-Towners look for a line of fabric, a contest, or a challenge and make a quilt specifically for that purpose. The group begins with a basic design or theme, which tends to change as they work on the quilt. "We do not know what the final quilt will look like until it's done!" Patty confesses.

For *Sunday Quilt,* they chose the Cocheco Reproduction Fabric Contest. The women tried to stay true to the era represented by the fabric and the New England style of the quilt by cutting out two corners, as if it was meant for a poster bed.

The project was a success. The quilt won first place at the Cocheco Contest at the American Textile History Museum in Lowell, Massachusetts. It has won many Best of Show and other awards and has even traveled around the world to Japan!

Note: Our staff rates this quilt as very challenging. It requires precise cutting and piecing, and keeping up with multiple units. Several pieces are also appliquéd. Please read the instructions in their entirety before beginning this quilt. We recommend this project for advanced quilters only.

Sunday Quilt

Finished Size

Quilt: 80" x 91"

Blocks: 4 (33" x 33") large medallions, 3 (13") small medallions

Materials

10 yards total assorted light yellow, white, and taupe prints for backgrounds

5 yards total assorted dark and medium prints for blocks and ribbon (purple, blue, pink, etc.)

1¼ yard gold-and-pink print for diamonds and rings

1½ yard green print for block diamonds and binding

7½ yards backing fabric

Full-size batting

Freezer paper

Cutting

Instructions are for rotary cutting and quick piecing. Patterns are on pages 95–96.

From assorted light yellow, white, and taupe prints, cut:

- Background: 16 (10¼") squares for corner units and 20 (10¼") squares for H pieces.
- 11 (10¾") squares. Cut squares in half diagonally to make 10 corner unit triangles and 12 arc unit triangles (I).
- 4 (10¼" x 11½") rectangles for bottom strip.
- 1 (14¼" x 11½") rectangle for center bottom piece.
- Large medallions: 4 (1⅞" x 42") assorted strips for Strip Set B.
- 16 (4⅝" x 22") strips for Strip Sets C and D.
- 4 (4⅝" x 42") strips for Es. Referring to *Diagram E,* cut

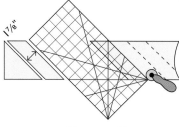

Diagram E

strips in 1⅞" increments to make 64 Es.

- Arc background pieces: 128 (2" x 2") squares for inner background.
- 128 (4" x 4") squares for outer background.
- Small medallion: 3 taupe centers (F). Fold 1 (5") square of freezer paper into quarters. Trace F on finished seam line and cut out. Place on folded square and trace arc. Cut on line to make F circle

appliqué pattern for small medallions. Repeat with 8" square for G rings for small medallions.

- 36 (2" x 2") taupe squares for inner background of small medallions.
- 36 (4" x 4") taupe squares for outer background of small medallions.
- 12 (2" x 2") yellow and white squares for inner points of center small medallion.
- 36 (2½" x 4") yellow and white pieces for outer points of small medallions.
- 1 taupe G ring for center small medallion.
- Ribbon background: 64 (4" x 4") squares.

From assorted dark and medium prints, cut:

- 4 sets of 2 (1⅞" x 22") dark star strips for Strip Set C.
- 16 (1⅞" x 42") dark strips in sets of 4 for Strip Set A.
- 16 (1⅞" x 42") medium strips in sets of 4 for Strip Sets A and B.
- 4 different sets of 8 Fs. Divide into groups of 4.
- 192 (1½" x 4") pieces for large medallion outer arc paper piecing in sets of 3.
- 96 (2" x 2") pieces for large medallion inner arc paper piecing.
- 24 assorted (2" x 2") pieces for inner arc paper piecing for small medallions in corners.
- 48 (2½" x 4") pieces for ribbon paper piecing.

From gold-and-pink print, cut:

- 4 (1⅞" x 42") strips. Cut strip set in half to make 8 strips for Strip Set D.
- 2 G rings for corner small medallions.
- 32 Gs for arc units.

From green print, cut:

- 8 (1⅞" x 42") strips. Cut strips in half to make 16 strips for Strip Sets C and D.
- 10 (2¼" x 42") strips for binding.

A Note on Color Placement

Color placement is important in this quilt to make the design pop! In the large medallions, each outer point of the star is the same gold print, and side diamonds are all the same green print. The purple medallion has alternating purple and blue in the arc sections, as does the blue medallion. The brown and pink medallions each also alternate colors in arcs. *Refer carefully to the photograph for inspiration.*

Large Medallion Assembly

1. Diamond assembly: Choose 1 light, 4 matching dark, and 4 matching medium strips for Strip Sets A and B.

2. Referring to *Strip Set A Diagram,* join 2 dark and 1 medium strips staggering ends as shown. Make 2 of Strip Set A. Trim left end to a 45° angle using markings on your ruler. Cut strip sets into 16 (1⅞"-wide) A segments.

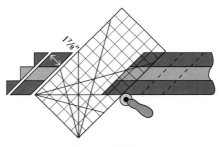

Strip Set A Diagram

3. Referring to *Strip Set B Diagram,* join 2 medium and 1 light strip, staggering ends, to make Strip Set B. Trim as above. Cut strip set into 8 (1⅞"-wide) B segments.

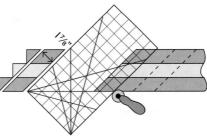

Strip Set B Diagram

4. Referring to *Nine-Patch Assembly Diagram,* lay out 2 A and 1 B segments. Join to make 1 Nine-Patch diamond. Make 8 Nine-Patch diamonds.

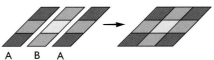

A   B   A

Nine-Patch Assembly Diagram

5. Choose 2 dark star strips, 4 green strips, 2 gold strips, and 4 different light strips for Strip Sets C and D.

6. Referring to *Strip Set C Diagram,* join 1 (1⅞" x 22") dark star strip, 1 (4⅝" x 22") light strip, and 1 (1⅞" x 22") green strip, staggering ends, to make 1 Strip Set C. Trim as above. Cut strip set into 4 (1⅞"-wide) C segments. Repeat with 1 star strip, different light strip, and 1 green strip for a total of 8 C segments.

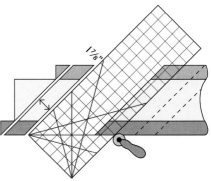

Strip Set C Diagram

7. Referring to *Strip Set D Diagram,* join 1 (1⅞" x 22") green strip, 1 (4⅝" x 22") light strip, and 1 (1⅞" x 22") gold strip, staggering ends, to make 1 Strip Set D. Trim as above. Cut strip set into 4 (1⅞"-wide) D segments. Repeat with 1 green strip, different light strip, and 1 gold strip for a total of 8 D segments.

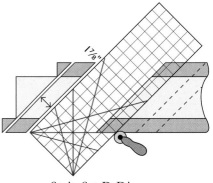

Strip Set D Diagram

8. Lay out 8 Nine-Patch diamonds, 8 C segments, 8 D segments, and 16 Es as shown in *Diamond Assembly Diagram*. Join as shown to make each diamond unit.

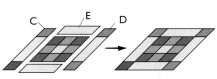

Diamond Assembly Diagram

Referring to *Large Medallion Assembly Diagram (see bottom of page),* join diamond units in pairs; join pairs to make star.

9. To assemble arc, choose 2 sets of 3 (1½" x 4") dark pieces for dark outer points and 4 (4" x 4") light pieces for background. Paper-piece outer arc, beginning with light for #1, 1 dark for #2, and second dark for #3. Keep the same point fabrics in the same arc positions for each arc. You may switch sides in

remaining arcs, but keep placement consistent within each arc *(Outer Arc Diagram)*. Make 8 outer arcs.

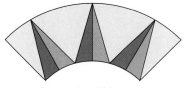

Outer Arc Diagram

10. Choose 3 dark and 4 light assorted (2" x 2") pieces for inner arc points. Paper-piece inner arc, beginning with light for #1 *(Inner Arc Diagram)*. Make 8 inner arcs.

Inner Arc Diagram

11. Referring to *Arc Assembly Diagram,* lay out 1 F, 1 inner arc, 1 G, and 1 outer arc. Working from inner point out, join seg-

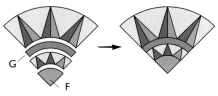

Arc Assembly Diagram

ments to make 1 arc unit. Blanket-stitch on both sides of G *(Blanket-Stitch Diagram)*. Make 8 arc units, 4 with 1 color F and 4 with second color F.

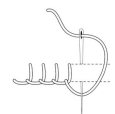

Blanket stitch Diagram

12. Note placement of square arc sections and triangle arc sections in medallion. Lay out arc units, squares, and triangles in position, alternating F fabrics.

13. Place 1 arc unit atop 1 H square, aligning raw edges. Appliqué arc to square to complete 1 square arc section *(Square Arc Diagram)*. Trim away excess on back. Make 5 square arc sections.

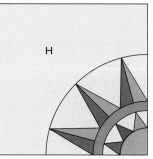

Square Arc Diagram

14. Place 1 arc unit atop 1 I triangle, aligning raw edges. Appliqué arc to triangle to complete 1 triangle arc section *(Triangle Arc Diagram)*. Trim away excess on back. Make 3 triangle arc sections.

Large Medallion Assembly Diagram

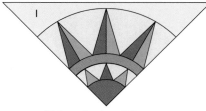

Triangle Arc Diagram

15. Referring to *Large Medallion Assembly Diagram (see bottom of previous page)*, set in square arc sections and triangle arc sections as shown, working in opposite pairs, to complete 1 large medallion *(Large Medallion Diagram—see bottom of this page)*. Make 4 large medallions.

Small Medallion Assembly

1. For center small medallion, choose 12 each yellow point pieces and taupe background 2" x 2" pieces. Paper-piece 4 inner arcs for small medallions.
2. Choose 12 each yellow and white (2½" x 4") point pieces and taupe background (4" x 4")

pieces. Paper-piece 4 outer arcs for small medallions.
3. Referring to *Inner Circle Diagram*, join 4 inner arcs to make circle. Appliqué taupe inner circle in center. Appliqué inner arc to taupe ring. Join 4 outer arcs to make outer circle. Appliqué ring to outer circle. Blanket-stitch on each side of ring to complete center medallion.

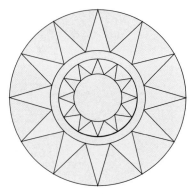

Inner Circle Diagram

4. Repeat to make 2 corner small medallions, replacing inner arc points with assorted medium prints and replacing taupe ring

with gold rings.
5. Baste edges under and press to prepare for appliqué.

Ribbon Assembly

1. Paper-piece 4 lights and 3 darks to make 1 ribbon unit *(Ribbon Unit Diagram)*. Do not trim end light pieces—leave extended beyond seam allowance.
2. Make 16 ribbon units.

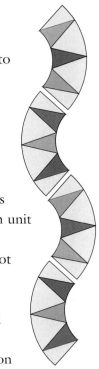

Ribbon Unit Diagram

Quilt Assembly

Refer to *Quilt Top Assembly Diagram* throughout.
1. Lay out 4 large medallions as shown and join, matching points. Appliqué yellow small medallion in center with points aligned like a clock face. Trim away behind appliqué, leaving ¼" seam allowance.
2. For top corners, join 4 (10¼") assorted squares to make 1 four-patch unit. Place four-patch unit on point and appliqué 1 corner small medallion in center. Trim away behind appliqué, leaving ¼" seam allowance. Add 3 triangles as shown to complete 1 top corner unit. Repeat for second top corner unit.
3. For bottom corners, join 4 (10¼") squares to make 1 four-patch. Add 2 triangles as shown to complete 1 bottom corner unit. Make 2 bottom corner units.
4. Set-in corner units to large medallion center.

Large Medallion Diagram

5. Join 4 (10¼" x 11½") rectangles and 1 (14¼" x 11½") rectangle to make bottom strip, large rectangle in center. Add to bottom of quilt.

6. Lay out ribbon sections on quilt top. You may need to extend ends of sections beyond paper piecing in order to fit ribbon as desired. When satisfied with placement, join sections to make ribbon. Place on quilt top to check placement and appliqué. (You may want to baste edges under and press before appliquéing.) Trim away behind ribbon, leaving ¼" seam allowance.

Quilting and Finishing

1. Divide backing fabric into 3 (2½-yard) lengths. Cut 1 piece in half lengthwise. Sew 1 narrow panel between wide panels. Press seam allowances toward narrow panel. Remaining panel is extra and may be used to make a hanging sleeve. Seams will run horizontally.

2. Layer backing, batting, and quilt top; baste. Quilt as desired. Quilt shown is quilted in-the-ditch in medallions with half feathers in outer diamonds. Ribbon and background feature feather swags, and are filled with windowpane grid work.

3. In each lower corner, cut out 1 (16" x 16") square as shown in *Trimming Diagram* for bedpost notches. Trim excess from blocks as indicated by red dashes.

4. Join 2¼"-wide green strips into 1 continuous piece for straight-grain French-fold binding. Add binding to quilt.

Quilt Top Assembly Diagram

Trimming Diagram

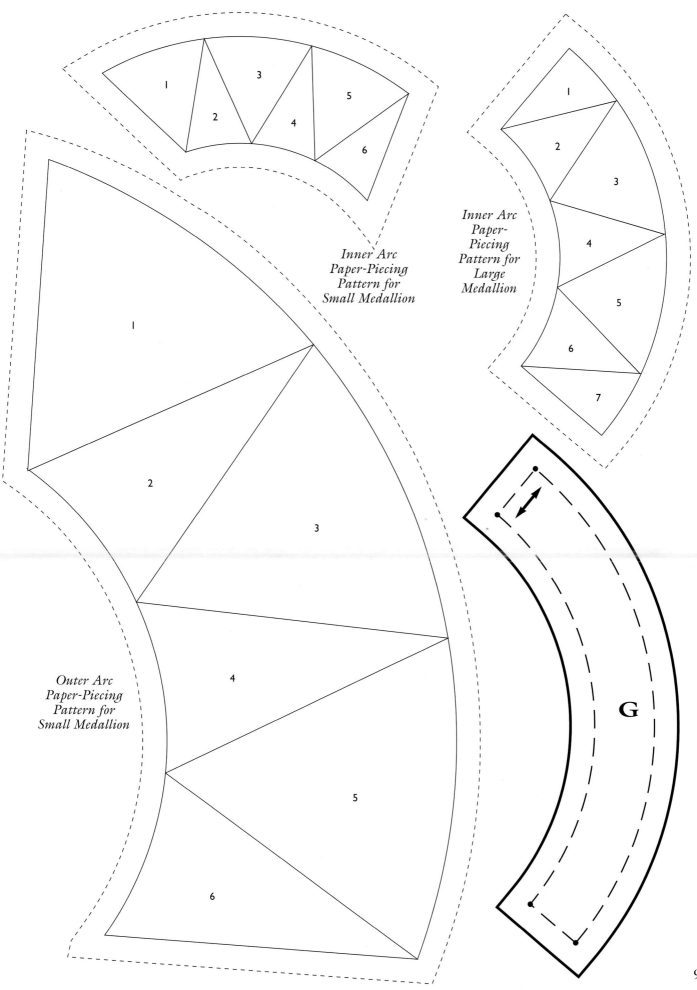

Inner Arc Paper-Piecing Pattern for Small Medallion

Inner Arc Paper-Piecing Pattern for Large Medallion

Outer Arc Paper-Piecing Pattern for Small Medallion

G

Paper Piecing

Place fabric #1 on wrong side of pattern, with wrong sides facing. Align fabric #2 with seam line so that it will flip over and cover area #2 after stitching. With right sides together, stitch along line between #1 and #2. Trim seam allowance, if needed, and flip #2 in place. Finger-press seam. Continue in numerical order. When paper pattern is complete, trim along seam allowance, remove paper, and press piece. For this quilt, do not trim the ends of the ribbon segments before removing paper.

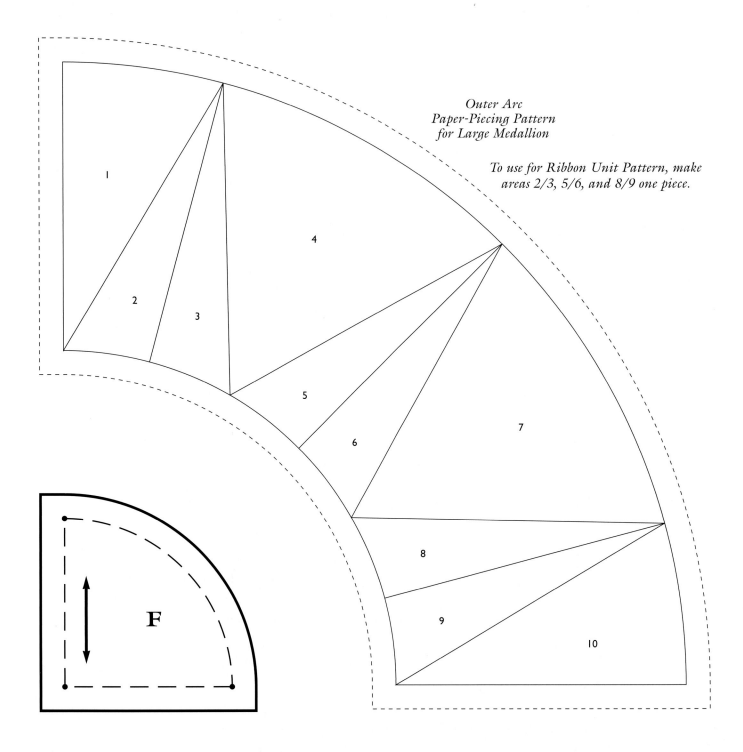

Outer Arc
Paper-Piecing Pattern
for Large Medallion

To use for Ribbon Unit Pattern, make
areas 2/3, 5/6, and 8/9 one piece.

Sharon Ann Waggoner & the Springfield Quilters Guild
Springfield, Illinois

Back Row: Cindy Pigg, Wanda Hummel, Carolyn Stine, Sharon Waggoner
Middle Row: Jan Wass, Rosie Evers, Judy Luecking, Mary Brown
Front Row: Marian Brockschmidt, Carlene Klickner, Elaine Eaton, Ann Aldrich

Sharon Ann Waggoner made her first quilt about 30 years ago. "My mother handed me a large bag of material left over from school clothes she had made for my sister, brother, and me," Sharon recalls. "My only 'lesson' was, 'Here, make a quilt!'"

The experience led to a life-long love of quilting. "I took classes in college for a

"We all learned something and grew as quilters with this pattern."

year and a half on watercolor painting and fabric design," says Sharon. "Creating new ideas and designs is exciting for me. I have way too many projects going on at one time, but I love to work on them all when time permits. My husband and two sons don't eat as well as they used to! I do sew more than I cook."

Sharon now belongs to the Springfield Quilters Guild and a smaller group, Four Friends for Fun. The Four Friends just finished their first round-robin quilt and are working on ideas for the next one.

Sharon joined the Springfield Quilters guild about three years ago. The guild started in 1984 and meets once a month. Through her involvement in the guild, the group made *Hidden Circles* for their 2002 raffle quilt.

Hidden Circles
2001

The Springfield Quilt Guild makes a raffle quilt every other year. Sharon Ann Waggoner and fellow guild member Kathy Jennings selected the *Hidden Circles* pattern, originally published in *Great American Quilts 1993*. They submitted the pattern to the guild for approval, and then had fun picking out the fabrics.

"Curves presented a challenge to all of us," says Sharon. She updated the instructions by making foundation paper-piecing patterns for the sharp points and distributing them to about 20 of the guild's 98 members. After receiving the pieced units back, Sharon attached all the background curves and pieced the blocks on point.

"We all learned something and grew as quilters with this pattern," says Sharon.

The quilt was part of a special Group Quilts display at the International Quilt Festival in Houston, Texas, in 2001. The quilt was later raffled in March 2002 at the Springfield Quilt Guild's quilt show.

Hidden Circles

Finished Size
Quilt: 84" x 101"
Blocks: 32 (12" x 12")

Materials
30 fat quarters (18" x 22") assorted prints for blocks
11 yards cream tone-on-tone print for blocks and border
1 fat eighth (9" x 22") blue print for appliqué
1 fat eighth (9" x 22") red print for appliqué
1 yard green print for appliqué
2 yards print for appliqué and binding
7½ yards backing fabric
Queen-size batting

Cutting
Patterns are on pages 101–103.
From assorted prints, cut:
- 64 sets of 2 matching As.
- 14 As.
- 32 sets of 4 matching 2" x 3" rectangles for block Bs.
- 32 sets of 4 matching 2" x 3" rectangles for block Bs.
- 28 (2" x 3") rectangles for side Bs.
- 32 sets of 4 matching 2" x 3" rectangles for block Cs.
- 32 sets of 4 matching 2" x 3" rectangles for block Cs.
- 28 (2" x 3") rectangles for side Cs.
- 32 sets of 4 matching Es.
- 14 Es.
- 32 sets of 4 matching Fs.
- 14 Fs.
- Sort into 32 sets for blocks: 2 sets of 2 matching As, 2 matching sets each of 4 Bs and 4 Cs, and 1 matching set each of 4 Es and 4 Fs.

- Sort into 14 sets for side setting triangles: 1 A, 2 Bs, 2 Cs, 1 E, 1 F.

From cream tone-on-tone print, cut:
- 3 yards. Cut yardage into 4 (8½"-wide) lengthwise strips for outer border.
- 22 (3"-wide) strips. Cut strips into 426 (2" x 3") rectangles for D areas.
- 128 Gs.
- 28 Hs.
- 3 (6⅞"-wide) strips. Cut strips into 14 (6⅞") squares. Cut squares in half diagonally to make 28 I triangles for side setting triangles. (You may use template I if you prefer.)
- 1 (12⅞"-wide) strip. Cut strip into 2 (12⅞") squares. Cut squares in half diagonally to make corner setting triangles.

From blue print, cut:
- 6 Ks.

From red print, cut:
- 6 Ls.

From green print, cut:
- 1 (18") square. From square, cut 270" of ¾"-wide bias strip. Cut strip into 8 (30"-long) strips for vines and 12 (1½"-long) strips for stems. Fold and press to make ¼"-wide appliqué vines and stems.
- 40 leaves: 14 M, 14 M reversed, 6 N, 6 N reversed.
- 16 Os.

From print, cut:

- 24 Js.
- 16 Ps.
- 1 (25") square. From square, cut 320" of 1½"-wide bias strip. Fold and press to make ½"-wide inner border appliqué bias strip.
- 1 (36") square. From square, cut 400" of 2¼"-wide bias strip for bias binding

Block Assembly

1. Trace or photocopy 142 arc patterns from page 102.

2. Choose 1 block set. Use foundation piecing to assemble 1 arc unit, using 2 Bs, 2 Cs, and 3 Ds. Make arc units, matching fabrics or assembling scrappy.

3. Referring to *Block Assembly Diagram 1,* join 1 arc unit with 1 each A, E, and F to make 1 block unit. Make 4 block units.

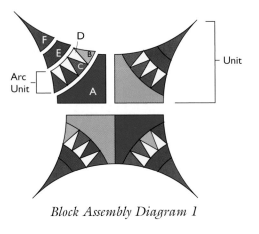

Block Assembly Diagram 1

4. Join 4 block units as shown in *Block Assembly Diagram 2.* Add G pieces to each side to complete 1 block. Make 32 blocks.

5. Make 1 block unit as above. Join 1 H to sides as shown in *Side Setting Triangle Block Diagram* to make 1 single unit. Add 1 I triangle to each side as shown to make 1 side setting triangle. Make 14 side setting triangles.

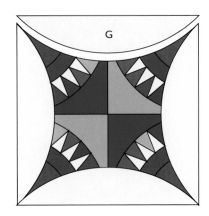

Block Assembly Diagram 2

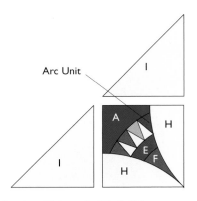

Setting Triangle Block Diagram

Quilt Assembly

1. Referring to *Quilt Top Assembly Diagram,* lay out blocks, side setting triangles, and corner triangles. Join into diagonal rows; join rows to complete center.

2. Add 1 border strip to each side of quilt. Miter corners.

3. Referring to photo, appliqué inner border bias strip, aligning inside edge with seam. On inner corners, use finished edge of Template G as a guide for inner edge.

4. Pin corner vines in place.

Quilt Top Assembly Diagram

Position stems and tuck under vines. Appliqué in place.

5. Gather 1 end of flower bud (P) under bud (O) as shown in *Bud Piecing Diagram*. Appliqué buds and leaves in place.

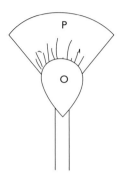

Bud Piecing Diagram

6. For corner flowers, place flower petals (J) and appliqué, overlapping as shown in *Border Flower Piecing Diagram*. Appliqué K and L in center. For side flowers, tuck stems under petals as shown

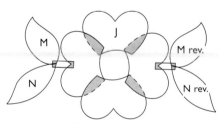

Border Flower Piecing Diagram

before appliquéing. Add leaves (M and N) to side flowers.

7. Each corner appliqué area has 2 vines, 2 stems, 4 flower bud units (P, O), 4 petals J, 1 K, 1 L, 3 M, 3 M rev., 1 N, and 1 N rev.

8. Each side flower has 2 stems, 1 each M and N, 1 each M and N rev., 4 Js, 1 K, and 1 L.

Quilting and Finishing

1. Divide backing fabric into 3 (2½-yard) lengths. Join along sides. Seams will run horizontally.

2. Layer backing, batting, and quilt top; baste. Quilt as desired. Quilt shown is outline-quilted around A pieces in blocks and has feather quilting to fill G areas. Appliqué on border is outline-quilted, with diagonal fill in border areas.

3. Round corners with a large dinner plate.

4. Join 2¼"-wide print strips into 1 continuous piece for bias French-fold binding. Add binding to quilt, stitching on drawn line for round corners. Trim excess quilt and complete binding.

A

M

H

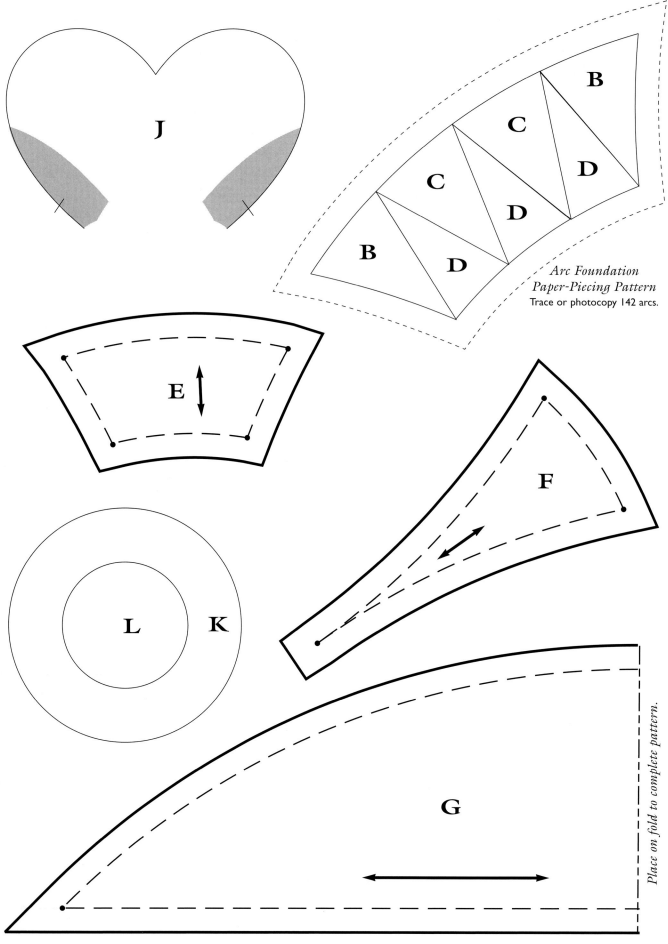

J

B
C
C
D
D
B
D

Arc Foundation
Paper-Piecing Pattern
Trace or photocopy 142 arcs.

E

F

L   K

G

Place on fold to complete pattern.

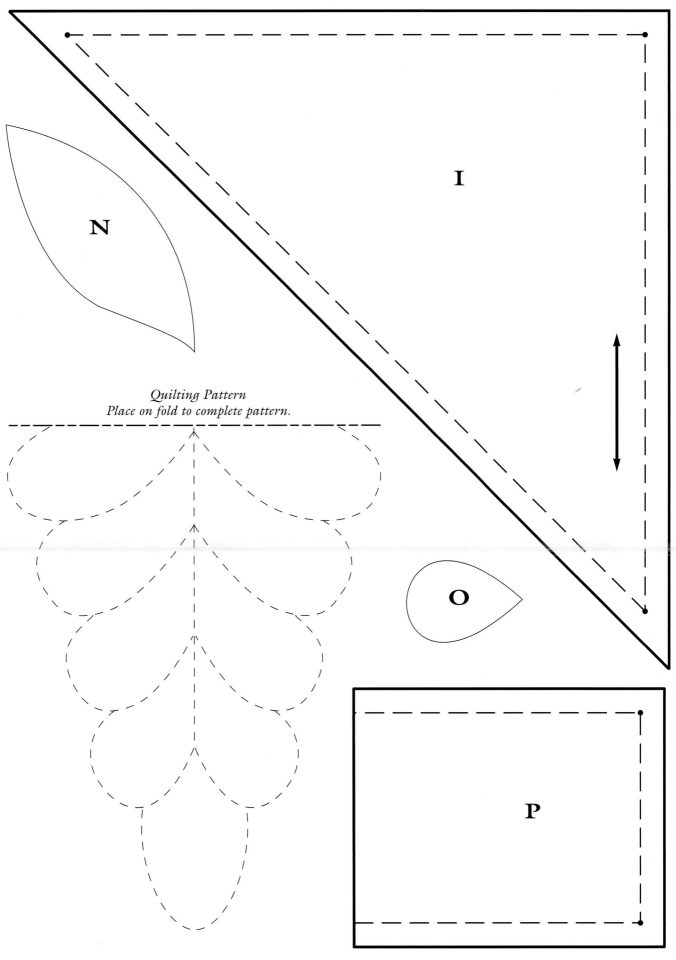

N

I

Quilting Pattern
Place on fold to complete pattern.

O

P

The Three of Us
Ozark, Missouri

*A*nita Sanker, Ethelyn Laughary, and Helen Johnson (shown left to right in adjacent photo) first met at their guild, the Ozark Piecemakers, in Springfield, Missouri. All three women had been sewing most of their lives and came to quilting 15 to 20 years ago. Their friendship developed quickly.

"As a group of three, it was a means of friendship and learning the art of quilting," says Helen Johnson. "We enjoyed trips to fabric stores, quilt shows, and classes, and we started meeting in each other's homes to quilt." The group has been together for 14 years, and they meet whenever they can.

"Quilting means friendship, creativity, and lots of sharing for us."

Athough Ethelyn Laughary moved to Westcliffe, Colorado, the group remains close. They still get together at least twice a year and stay in touch through phone calls and letters. "Quilting means friendship, creativity, and lots of sharing for us," says Helen.

The three also belong to the Calico Cutups in Forsyth, Missouri. Since moving, Ethelyn also belongs to the Royal Gorge Quilt Council in Canyon City, Colorado, and the Olde Schoolhouse Quilters in Westcliffe, Colorado.

Springtime Dogwoods in the Ozarks
2000

Before making *Springtime Dogwood in the Ozarks*, Helen says, "Our goal was to see if we could create a quilt and have it accepted into the American Quilter's Society Show in Paducah."

Anita and Ethelyn are dedicated appliquérs, while Helen prefers piecing. Ethelyn appliquéd the center medallion, Helen pieced the dogwood blocks, and Anita appliquéd the borders. Anita and Helen assembled the quilt pieces into a completed top.

Ethelyn started quilting the center, and then had to move to Colorado. During her transition, Anita and Helen quilted, and then sent the quilt back to Ethelyn for completion. They finished it in August 2000—just in time for the Ozark Piecemakers Quilt Show in September.

All their hard work paid off. The quilt won Honorable Mention in the Ozark show. It won another Honorable Mention at the Indiana Heritage Quilt Show in February 2001, and took home both Viewer's Choice and Best of Show at the Calico Cutups Quilt Show in Forsyth, Missouri.

And just as they had dreamed, the quilt was juried into the American Quilter's Society Show at Paducah, Kentucky, in April 2001. It was also juried into the National Quilter's Association Quilt Show in Tulsa, Oklahoma.

So how do these three women decide who gets to keep this prize-winning quilt?

"We each get to keep the quilt for a year," says Ethelyn. "This year is my year!"

Springtime Dogwoods in the Ozarks

Finished Size
Quilt: 96" x 108"
Blocks: 22 (12" x 12")

Materials
Note: In quilt shown, all fabrics are batiks except green print.

$6\frac{1}{2}$ yards light blue for background and border

$1\frac{1}{2}$ yards red for border, piping, and appliqué

3 yards light green for border, blocks, and leaves

4 yards dark green for borders and leaves

$3\frac{1}{2}$ yards white-with-pink for dogwood blossoms

$1\frac{3}{4}$ yards dark blue for outer border and binding

$1\frac{3}{4}$ yards dark green print for vines and stems

1 fat quarter (18" x 22") gold print for dogwood centers

3" x 10" piece light brown for branch

2" x 5" piece black print for legs

2" x 3" piece black for face and eye

2" x 2" piece gold for beak

9 yards backing fabric

King-size batting

White embroidery floss

Cutting
Instructions are for rotary cutting and quick piecing. Border strips are exact length needed. You may want to cut them longer to allow for piecing variations. Patterns are on pages 109–111. **Cut pieces in order listed to make best use of yardage.**

From light blue, cut:
- 1 (40" x 52") piece for background.
- 10 ($7\frac{1}{2}$"-wide) strips. Piece strips to make 2 ($7\frac{1}{2}$" x $90\frac{1}{2}$") side borders and 2 ($7\frac{1}{2}$" x $92\frac{1}{2}$") top and bottom borders.
- 6 ($2\frac{1}{2}$"-wide) strips. Cut strips into 88 ($2\frac{1}{2}$") squares for dogwood blocks.
- 22 ($2\frac{1}{2}$"-wide) strips. Cut strips into 176 ($2\frac{1}{2}$" x $4\frac{1}{2}$") rectangles for leaf units.
- 6 ($2\frac{1}{2}$"-wide) strips. Cut strips into 88 ($2\frac{1}{2}$") squares for petal units.

From red, cut:
- 5 ($1\frac{1}{2}$"-wide) strips. Piece strips as needed to make 2 ($1\frac{1}{2}$" x $50\frac{1}{2}$") side borders and 2 ($1\frac{1}{2}$" x $40\frac{1}{2}$")

top and bottom borders.
- 12 (1"-wide) strips. Piece to make 2 (1" x $104\frac{1}{2}$") side piping strips and 2 (1" x 93") top and bottom piping strips. Fold in half lengthwise, wrong sides together, to make piping.
- For bird: 1 each G, H, I, J, K, L, M, N.
- For tulips: 10 Os and 8 Ys from lighter areas, 10 Ps and 8 Zs from darker areas.

From light green, cut:
- 5 (2"-wide) strips. Piece strips to make 2 (2" x $52\frac{1}{2}$") side borders and 2 (2" x $43\frac{1}{2}$") top and bottom borders.
- 18 (2"-wide) strips. Cut strips into 176 (2" x 4") rectangles for petal units.

- 14 (2"-wide) strips. Cut strips into 176 (2" x 3") rectangles for leaf units.
- 41 small dogwood leaves T. Leaves vary in size and shape; you may substitute dark and light green as you desire.
- 12" x 12" piece for lined tulip leaves.

From dark green, cut:
- 6 (3"-wide) strips. Piece strips to make 2 (3" x 55½") side borders and 2 (3" x 48½") top and bottom borders.
- 9 (3½"-wide) strips. Piece strips to make 2 (3½" x 84½") side borders and 2 (3½" x 78½") top and bottom borders.
- 68 small dogwood leaves (T).
- 24 large dogwood leaves (S).
- 12" x 12" piece for lined tulip leaves.
- 5 large tulip leaves (Q).
- 10 small tulip leaves (R).

From white with pink, cut:
- 11 (4½"-wide) strips. Cut strips into 88 (4½") squares for pieced dogwood blossom area #1.
- 80 small petals.
- 164 large petals. Dogwood petals vary in size and shape; vary as desired.

From dark blue, cut:
- 11 (2½"-wide) strips. Piece strips to make 2 (2½" x 104½") side borders and 2 (2½" x 96½") top and bottom borders.
- 11 (2¼"-wide) strips for binding.

From dark green print, cut:
- 1 (25") square. Make 500" of ¾"-wide bias strip. Cut bias strip into 1 (70"-long) piece for center circle and 4 (100"-long) strips for border vines. Fold and press to make ¼"-wide bias.
- 1 (30") square. Make 430" of

1⅛" bias strip. Cut bias strip into 4 (100" long) strips for border vines and 2 (6"-long) pieces for tulip stems. Fold and press to make ⅜"-wide bias.

From gold print, cut:
- 22 pieced block centers, 1¾" diameter finished.
- 41 large centers (W).
- 20 small centers (X). Centers vary with size of dogwood.

From light brown, cut:
- 1 branch (A).

From black print, cut:
- 1 each B and C for legs.

From black, cut:
- 1 face (D).
- 1 eye (E).

From gold, cut:
- 1 beak (F).

Center Applique

Refer to photo throughout.

1. Using a pencil tied to a string, draw a 22"-diameter circle centered on background. Pin vine in place for center circle. Appliqué in place.

2. Place and appliqué in order: branch (A), legs (B) and (C), face (D), eye (E), beak (F), crest (G), head (H), breast (I), tail (J), wing (K), and wing details (L, M, and N). Backstitch circle on eye in white.

Backstitch Diagram

3. Prepare lined tulip leaves: place dark green and light green pieces together, right sides facing. Cut 3 large and 2 small tulip leaf pairs. Do not separate. Stitch, leaving base open. Trim seam allowance; turn from leaf base. These will be appliquéd in place with the tip flipped over as shown in photo. One each large and small leaves will be used in border appliqué.

4. Place and appliqué in order: for left tulip—1 lined large leaf (Q), 1 large leaf (Q), 1 tulip stem, 1 large tulip bottom (O), 1 large tulip top (P). For right tulip—1 tulip stem, 1 large lined tulip leaf (Q), 1 small lined tulip leaf (R), 1 small tulip leaf (R), 1 bottom O, 1 top (P).

5. Place center dogwood blossoms and appliqué: leaves, petals, and centers. Center leaves vary in size and color; refer to photo. Around center circle, there are 5 large dogwoods at bottom, with 12 leaves. Base of left tulip is covered by 1 small dogwood blossom with 3 leaves. Two large dogwoods with 7 leaves are at top left, and circle top has 1 large and 2

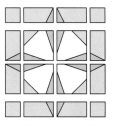

Block Assembly Diagram

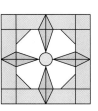

Block Diagram

small blossoms with 8 leaves. Right tulip base is covered with 1 large dogwood with 4 leaves.

6. Place corner dogwood blossoms and appliqué: leaves, petals, and centers. Each corner has 3 large blossoms and 6 large leaves.

7. Trim center to 38½" x 50½".

Dogwood Block Assembly

1. Trace or photocopy paper piecing patterns. You will need 88 petals, 88 left leaves, and 88 right leaves.

2. Paper-piece 1 petal of dogwood block using pink and white batik for #1, green for #2 and #3, and blue for #4. Repeat to make 4 petals.

3. Paper-piece 1 leaf unit using blue for #1 and green for #2. Make 4 with green on right and 4 with green on left.

4. Remove paper from units and press.

5. Referring to *Block Assembly Diagram*, lay out 4 petals, 8 leaf units, and 4 blue squares. Join to make 1 Dogwood block *(Block Diagram)*. Appliqué 1 gold center to center of block.

6. Make 22 Dogwood blocks.

Quilt Assembly

Refer to *Quilt Top Assembly Diagram* throughout.

1. Add inner red side borders to center appliquéd block. Add inner top and bottom borders.

2. Add light green side borders to

quilt. Add top and bottom borders.

3. Add dark green side borders to quilt. Add top and bottom borders.

4. Join 5 Dogwood blocks to make 1 side border. Repeat to make 2 side borders. Add to quilt.

5. Join 6 Dogwood blocks to make top border. Repeat for bottom border. Add to quilt, matching seams.

6. Add dark green outer side borders to quilt. Add top and bottom borders.

7. Add light blue side borders to quilt. Add top and bottom borders.

8. Baste red side piping in place. Add dark blue outer side borders.

9. Baste red top and bottom piping in place. Tuck ends inside fold to match width of side piping; this

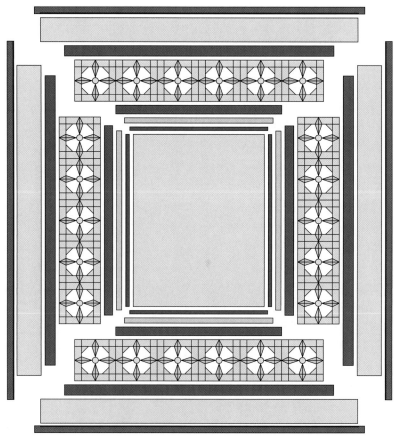

Quilt Top Assembly Diagram

108

finishes ends of top and bottom strips. Add dark blue top and bottom borders.

10. Pin in place on blue border: 1 (⅜"-wide) vine and 1 (¼"-wide) vine on each side, crossing as shown. Trim excess. When satisfied with placement, appliqué in place.

11. Appliqué dogwoods, leaves, and tulips onto border. Top border has 2 large dogwoods, 4 small dogwoods, 2 small tulips, and 15 leaves. Top right corner has 2 large tulips, 1 small lined tulip leaf, 2 small tulip leaves, 1 large tulip leaf, 1 large dogwood, 2 small dogwoods, and 5 leaves. Right border has 4 large dogwoods, 2 small dogwoods, 2 small tulips, and 12 leaves. Right bottom corner has 1 large lined tulip leaf, 3 small tulip leaves, 2 large tulips, 2 large dogwoods, 1 small dogwood, and 5 leaves.

12. Bottom border has 3 large dogwoods, 3 small dogwoods, 2 small tulips, and 15 leaves. Bottom left corner has 4 large tulip leaves, 2 large tulips, 3 large dogwoods, and 5 leaves. Left border has 4 large dogwoods, 2 small dogwoods, 2 small tulips, and 12 leaves. Top left corner has 4 small tulip leaves, 2 large tulips, 1 large dogwood, 2 small dogwoods, and 7 leaves.

Quilting and Finishing

1. Divide backing fabric into 3 (3-yard) lengths. Join along sides to make backing. Seams will run horizontally.

2. Layer backing, batting, and quilt top; baste. Quilt as desired. Quilt shown is outline-quilted around appliqué. Center block is filled with a 1" grid, and narrow borders have a chain pattern. Outer border has diagonal fill.

3. Join 2¼"-wide blue strips into 1 continuous piece for straight-grain French-fold binding. Add binding to quilt.

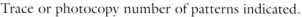

Dogwood Center Circle

Trace or photocopy number of patterns indicated.

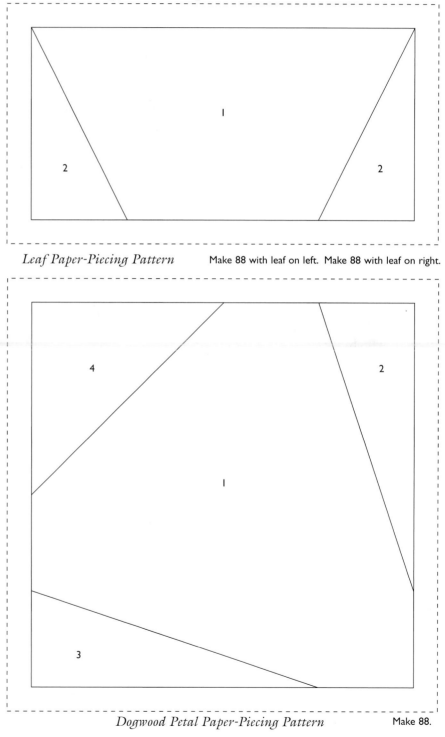

Leaf Paper-Piecing Pattern   Make **88** with leaf on left. Make **88** with leaf on right.

Dogwood Petal Paper-Piecing Pattern   Make **88**.

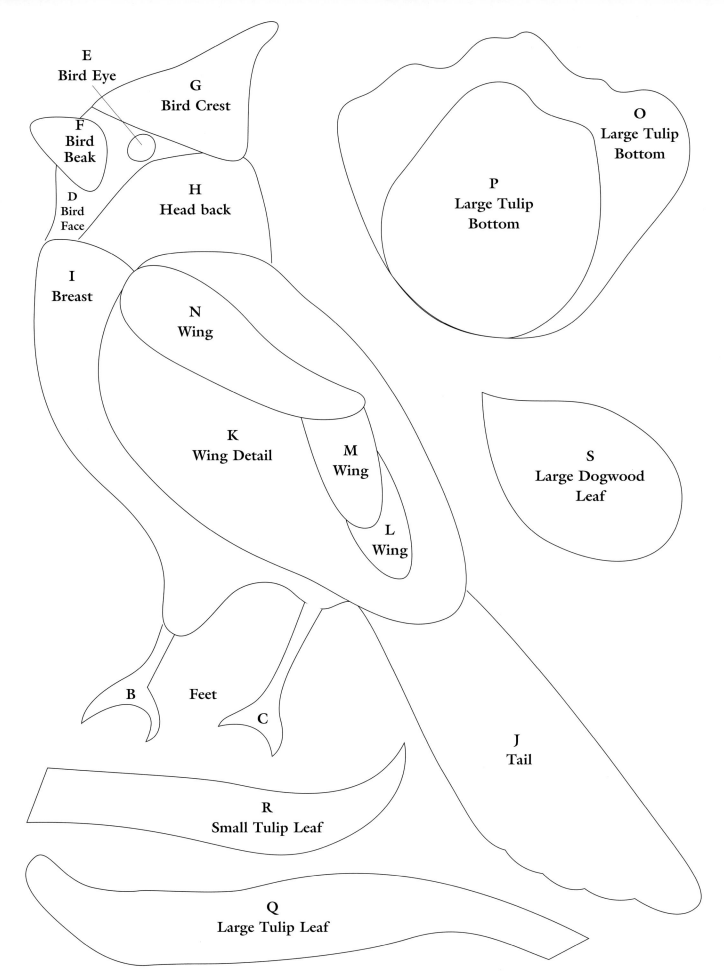

E
Bird Eye

G
Bird Crest

F
Bird
Beak

D
Bird
Face

H
Head back

O
Large Tulip
Bottom

P
Large Tulip
Bottom

I
Breast

N
Wing

K
Wing Detail

M
Wing

L
Wing

S
Large Dogwood
Leaf

B   Feet

C

J
Tail

R
Small Tulip Leaf

Q
Large Tulip Leaf

110

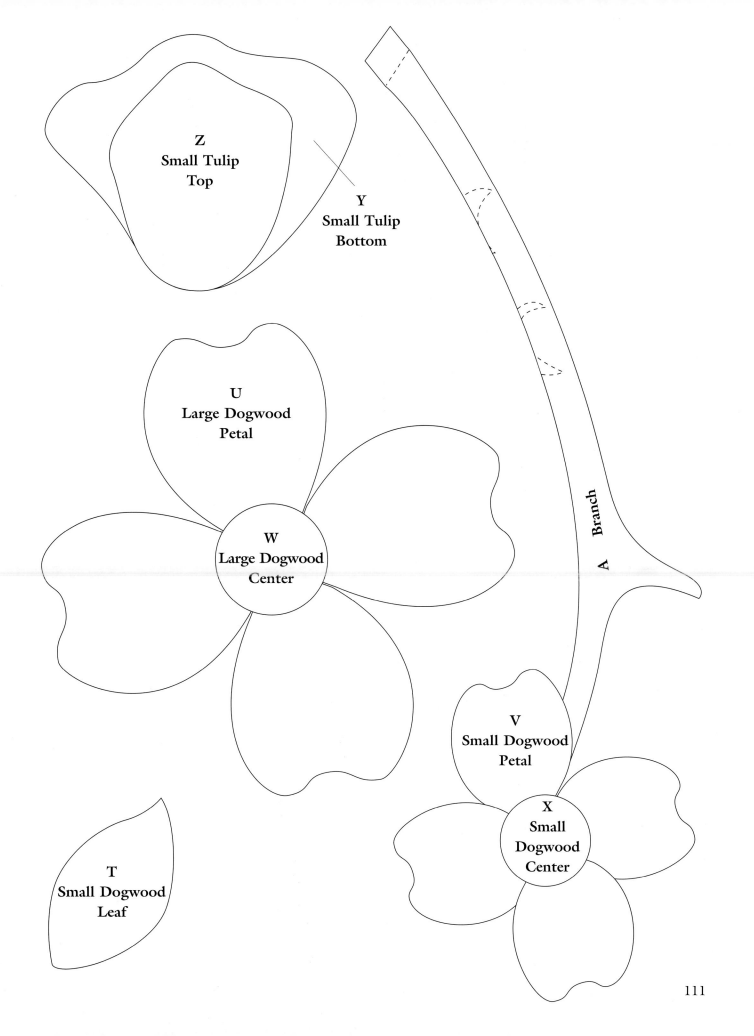

Z
Small Tulip
Top

Y
Small Tulip
Bottom

U
Large Dogwood
Petal

W
Large Dogwood
Center

V
Small Dogwood
Petal

X
Small
Dogwood
Center

A Branch

T
Small Dogwood
Leaf

111

Ruth Powers & Kansas Capital Quilt Guild
Carbondale, Kansas

*R*uth Powers began quilting in 1989 because she wanted a wall hanging for her new home. "I didn't expect to enjoy the process, but I was very surprised that I did enjoy all aspects of it, from designing the quilt to the hand quilting."

Ruth soon joined the Kansas Capital Quilt Guild and learned even more. By 1993, she was president. *Words of Wisdom* is the collective result of blocks made by her fellow guild members. Ruth is also a member of the Kaw Valley Quilt Guild, Quilt Buddies, Grapevine Quilters, and the Kansas Art Quilters.

"Quilting dominates my life now!" Ruth confesses. "In 1994, I started my own pattern company for quilts and wall hangings called Innovations. I love to make pieces for competitions as well, but I find that the business takes up so much of my time, it is difficult to meet show deadlines."

Nonetheless, Ruth's work has appeared in national juried shows. Although Ruth hand-quilted all of her projects in the early years, she now machine-quilts most projects to meet show and business deadlines.

To see more of Ruth's quilts, visit her Web site at: www.innovationsquilts.com

"Quilting dominates my life now!"

Words of Wisdom
1996

The block Ruth Powers used to make this quilt is actually called Four Squares. "I loved how, when put together, the corners formed stars," says Ruth.

Ruth was president of the Kansas Capital Quilters Guild in Topeka, Kansas in 1993.

"It is a guild tradition to make blocks for the outgoing president," Ruth says. "I drafted the pattern and requested that my blocks be made in any shade of red, plus white or white-on-white fabric. I asked that each person sign the central square and add an upbeat message. *Words of Wisdom* seemed an appropriate name!"

Although most of the blocks were machine-pieced, a few were hand-pieced.

"I enjoyed reading the messages and thinking about the makers of each block as I did the hand quilting," Ruth recalls.

The quilt was exhibited at the Kansas Capital Quilt Guild Show in 1996 and the Maple Leaf Festival.

Words of Wisdom

Finished Size
Quilt: 84" x 96"
Blocks: 56 (12" x 12")

Materials

56 fat quarters (18" x 22") assorted
  red prints {or 56 (10" x 22")
  pieces}
56 fat eighths (9" x 22") assorted
  white on white prints (4¼
  yards if using same light print
  in all blocks)
¾ yard red print for binding
7½ yards backing fabric
Queen-size batting

Cutting

Instructions are for rotary cutting
and quick piecing. Pattern is on
page 115. **Cut pieces in order
listed to make best use of
yardage.**

From each red print, cut:
• 1 (5¼") square. Cut square in
  quarters diagonally to make 4 B
  triangles.
• 4 Ds.
• 4 Ds reversed.

From each white on white print, cut:
• 1 (4½") A square.
• 1 (5¼") square. Cut square in
  quarters diagonally to make 4 B
  triangles.
• 2 (4⅞") squares. Cut squares
  in half diagonally to make 4 C
  triangles.

If using same light print in all blocks:
• Cut 7 (4½" x 42") strips. Cut
  strips into 56 (4½") A squares.
• Cut 8 (5¼" x 42") strips. Cut
  strips into 56 (5¼") squares.
  Cut squares in quarters diagonally to make 224 B triangles.

• Cut 14 (4⅞" x 42") strips. Cut
  strips into 112 (4⅞") squares.
  Cut squares in half diagonally to
  make 224 C triangles.

From red print, cut:
• 10 (2¼" x 42") strips for
  binding.

Block Assembly

Refer to *Block Assembly Diagram*
throughout.

1. Choose 1 red and 1 white set.
Join 1 red B triangle to each opposite side of 1 white A square.
Join 1 red B triangle to remaining sides.

2. Join 1 white C triangle to each opposite side of A/B unit. Join
1 white C triangle to remaining sides.

3. Join 1 red D and 1 red D rev. to sides of 1 white B triangle to
make side strip. Make 4 side strips. Add to center, matching B triangle
points. Set in corner seams to complete 1 block.

4. Make 56 blocks. Note that in top corner blocks, 1 red D and 1 red D rev. are replaced with

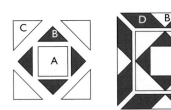

Block Assembly Diagram

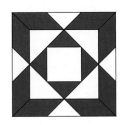

Block Diagram

white prints. You may duplicate this look exactly, or use red pieces to make all four quilt corners the same. Blocks shown are signed in center square. Blocks should be signed before assembling the quilt top.

Quilt Assembly

1. Lay out blocks in 8 horizontal rows of 7 blocks each.
2. Join blocks into rows; join rows to complete quilt.

Quilting and Finishing

1. Divide backing fabric into 3 (2½-yard) lengths. Cut 1 piece in half lengthwise. Sew 1 narrow panel between wide panels. Press seam allowances toward narrow panel. Remaining panel is extra and may be used to make a hanging sleeve. Seams will run horizontally.
2. Layer backing, batting, and quilt top; baste. Quilt as desired.

As is sometimes the case in group quilts, Ruth received more blocks than would fit mathematically on the front. So she put her blocks, any duplicates, and unsigned blocks on the back.

Quilt shown is quilted in diagonals in stars.
3. Join 2¼"-wide red strips and random red strips into 1 continuous piece for straight-grain French-fold binding. Add binding to quilt.

Quilt Top Assembly Diagram

D

Little Quilts
Marietta, Georgia

Collectively, Alice Berg, Sylvia Johnson, and Mary Ellen Von Holt (shown left to right in adjacent photo) make up Little Quilts®. These partners work as a team, combining their talents to produce their own quilt patterns and booklets and design fabrics for Peter Pan Fabrics.

"The three of us met through the East Cobb Quilters Guild, of which we are still active members," says Sylvia.

Little Quilts began in 1984 by selling ready-made reproduction doll quilts that were used to decorate homes. These collectibles were displayed on walls, in baskets, or with collections. High demand led the women to start making kits and patterns for those who wished to make their own quilts.

"Little Quilts projects are meant to be fun and carefree."

"Our quilts are not miniature quilts," says Mary Ellen, "but rather small quilts based on traditional designs from days gone by."

In 1998, the three women opened their own retail store in a building that formerly served as an old mill. The setting is perfect for their signature folk-art look. In addition to fabric and quilting kits, the store offers gifts, pottery, wool, rug hooking supplies and kits, and stitchery items.

"Little Quilts projects are meant to be fun and carefree," says Alice. "Don't worry about perfection! If the seams don't match and the appliqué stitches show, give the quilt a strong tea bath and tell your friends, 'Look at this old doll quilt I made when I was ten years old—we found it in the attic!'"

Homecoming
1998

"Our quilts are designed to use many fabrics, just as quilts from the 19th century were made," says Alice. "Because we like scrap quilts, we use many different fabrics in small quantities."

Although we give specific yardages for the quilt in the instructions, you may wish to pull bits from your scrap basket to create your own look.

"This folksy quilt is full of patchwork fun," Alice says. "The appliquéd crows and simple embroidery were inspired by traditional antique quilts and our sense of whimsy."

Little Quilts
1450-C Roswell Road
Marietta, GA 30062
(770) 578-6727
www.littlequilts.com

Homecoming

Finished Size
Quilt: 30" x 40"
Blocks: 1 (15" x 15"), 8 (5" x 5")

Materials
Assorted small scraps red, blue brown, gold, green, tan, etc. See photo for inspiration.
1 (9" x 22") fat eighth light print for center square background
½ yard red print for center square and binding
¼ yard tan plaid for embroidery and fill blocks
⅜ yard solid black for border and crows
½ yard green print for border
1 yard fabric for backing
1 (31" x 41") piece batting
Black embroidery floss
2 small black buttons

Cutting
Instructions are for rotary cutting and quick piecing. Border strips are exact length needed. You may want to make them longer to allow for piecing variations. Patterns are on page 121.
Cut pieces in order listed to make best use of yardage.
From assorted small scraps, cut:
- 7 (2⅞") green squares. Cut squares in half diagonally to make 14 green A triangles for tree.
- 1 (3½") green E square for tree.
- 1 (6½") brown C square for trunk.
- 1 (3½") brown E square for trunk section.
- 36 (1½") assorted G squares. You will need 8 assorted, 9 dark, and 9 light for Framed Nine-Patch blocks, 4 dark for

Half-Tree blocks, and 6 light for House windows.
- 2 sets of 4 matching (1½" x 3½") green H strips for Framed Nine-Patch blocks.
- 6 background sets of 5 matching light (1½") G squares for House blocks.
- 6 roof sets of matching 2 (1½") G squares and 1 (1½" x 5½") I rectangle for House blocks.
- 6 house sets of matching 2 (1½") G squares, 1 (1½" x 3½") H rectangles, 1 (1½" x 5½") I rectangle, and 1 (1½" x 2½") J rectangle for House blocks.
- 6 (1½" x 2½") assorted light J rectangles for doors in House blocks.
- 4 (2⅞") assorted squares. Cut squares in half diagonally to make 4 sets of 2 A triangles for Half-Tree blocks.
- 52 (1¾") assorted K squares for Four-Patch blocks.
- 10 (2¾") assorted gold and tan squares. Cut squares in half diagonally to make 20 L triangles for Four-Patch blocks.
- 4 (4¾") assorted gold and tan squares. Cut squares in quarters diagonally to make 16 M triangles for Four-Patch blocks.
- 4 (1¼" x 4") gold or tan coping strips (N) for Quad Four-Patch units.
- 2 (4" x 3") gold or tan P rectangles.

From light print, cut:
- 1 (5½" x 22") strip. Cut strip into 2 (5½") D squares. From remainder, cut 2 (2½") B squares.
- 1 (2⅞" x 22") strip. Cut strip into 7 (2⅞") squares. Cut squares in half diagonally to make 14 A triangles for tree.

From red print, cut:
- 1 (8" x 42") strip. Cut strip into 2 (8") squares. Cut squares in half diagonally to make 4 F triangles.
- 4 (2¼" x 42") strips for binding.

From tan plaid, cut:
- 1 (4" x 42") strip. Cut strip into 1 (4" x 7½") O rectangle, 1 (4" x 6") Q rectangle, and 1 (4" x 9½") R rectangle.

From solid black for border and crows, cut:
- 2 (1" x 42") strips. Cut strips into 4 (1" x 16") strips for center block border.
- 4 (1½" x 42") strips. Cut

strips into 2 (1½" x 32½") inner side borders and 2 (1½" x 24½") inner top and bottom borders.

- 2 crows.

From green print, cut:

- 4 (3½" x 42") strips. Cut strips into 2 (3½" x 34½") outer side borders and 2 (3½" x 30½") outer top and bottom borders.

Block Assembly

Tree Block

A Unit Assembly Diagram

1. Referring to *A Unit Assembly Diagram*, join 1 light and 1 green A triangles to make 1 A unit. Make 14 A units.
2. Referring to *Tree Trunk Diagram 1*, lightly draw a line from corner to corner on wrong side of 2 light print D squares. Place 1 light D square atop 1 corner of brown C square, right sides facing. Using diagonal seams, stitch along line. Trim excess fabric ¼" from stitching and press open. Repeat on opposite side to make trunk.

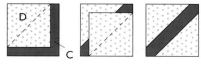

Tree Trunk Diagram 1

3. Place 1 green E square on 1 corner of trunk unit as shown in *Tree Trunk Diagram 2*. Using diagonal seams, stitch along line. Trim excess fabric ¼" from stitching and press open. Repeat

Tree Trunk Diagram 2

with 1 brown E square on opposite end of trunk to complete trunk section.

4. Referring to *Tree Block Assembly Diagram*, lay out trunk section, 2 light print B squares, and 14 A units. Join into sections. Join sections to complete inner tree block.

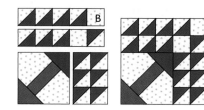

Tree Block Assembly Diagram

5. Join 1 F to each side of inner tree block to complete center tree block *(Tree Block Diagram)*.

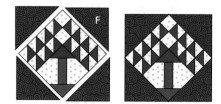

Tree Block Diagram

6. Add side black borders to block. Press and trim excess length. Add top and bottom black borders. Press and trim block to 15½" square, if needed.

Framed Nine-Patch Assembly

1. Choose 5 dark and 4 light G squares. Referring to *Nine-Patch Assembly Diagram*, lay out in 3 horizontal rows of 3 squares each. Join into rows; join rows to complete Nine-Patch.

Nine-Patch Assembly Diagram

2. Choose 4 matching H strips and 4 G squares. Referring to *Framed Nine-Patch Block Assembly Diagram*, add 1 H strip

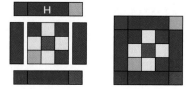

Framed Nine-Patch Assembly Diagram

to each side of block. Add 1 G square to ends of remaining H strips. Add to top and bottom to complete 1 Framed Nine-Patch block.

3. Repeat, using 5 light and 4 dark G squares, to make second Framed Nine-Patch block.

House Block Assembly

Refer to *House Block Assembly Diagram* throughout.

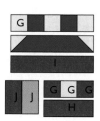

House Block Assembly Diagram

1. Choose 1 background set (5 light Gs), 1 roof set (1 I, 2 Gs), 1 house set (2 Gs, 1 H, 1 I, 1 J), 1 door (1 light J) and 1 window (1 light G).
2. Alternate 3 background Gs and 2 roof Gs to make top strip.
3. Referring to *Diagonal Seams Diagram*, place 1 background G on 1 end of roof I strip. Stitch along drawn line. Trim excess fabric ¼" from stitching and press open. Repeat on opposite end to complete second strip. Join to top strip to make roof unit.

Diagonal Seams Diagram

4. Join house J and door J to make left unit. Join 2 house Gs and 1 window G as shown. Join to top of house H to make right unit. Join left and right units. Add house I to make house unit.

119

5. Join roof and house units to complete 1 House block (*House Block Diagram*).

House Block Diagram

6. Make 6 House blocks.

Half-Tree Block Assembly

1. Choose 2 sets of matching A triangles and 2 G squares. Referring to *Half-Tree Block Assembly Diagram*, join 1 each of A triangles to make 1 A unit. Make 2 A units. Join as shown. Join 2 G squares and add to top of A units to make top Half-Tree block.

Half-Tree Block Assembly Diagram

2. Repeat to make bottom Half-Tree block, placing G squares at bottom.

Four-Patch Assembly

1. Referring to *Four-Patch Assembly Diagram*, join 4 K squares to make 1 Four-Patch unit. Make 13 Four-Patch blocks.

Four-Patch Assembly Diagram

2. Referring to *Single Four-Patch Assembly Diagram*, join 4 L triangles to each side of 1 Four-Patch block to make 1 Single Four-Patch block. Trim to 4".

Single Four-Patch Assembly Diagram

3. Referring to *Double Four-Patch Assembly Diagram*, join 4 L triangles, 2 M triangles, and 2

Double Four-Patch Assembly Diagram

Four-Patch blocks to make 1 Double Four-Patch unit. Make 2 double units.

4. Referring to *Quad Four-Patch Assembly Diagram*, join 4 L triangles, 6 M triangles, and 4 Four-Patch blocks as shown.

Quad Four-Patch Assembly Diagram

Add 1 (1¼" x 4") coping strip to each end to make 1 Quad Four-Patch unit. Make 2 Quad units. Quad units should measure 4" x 15½".

Embroidered Blocks

1. On O rectangle, back stitch 1 star using three strands of black embroidery floss.

2. On R rectangle, embroider "Home" using three strands of black embroidery floss.

Quilt Assembly

Refer to *Quilt Top Assembly Diagram* throughout.

1. Work from top to bottom. For first row, lay out O rectangle, 1 Double Four-Patch block, 1 P, and Q. Join to make first row.

2. For second row, lay out 3 House blocks, top Half-Tree

Quilt Top Assembly Diagram

120

block, and 1 Framed Nine-Patch block as shown. Join to make second row.

3. For third row, join 1 Quad Four-Patch block to each side of center Tree block.

4. For fourth row, lay out Framed Nine-Patch block, 3 House blocks, and bottom Half-Tree block as shown. Join to make fourth row.

5. For fifth row, lay out 1 P, R, 1 Single, and 1 Double Four-Patch block as shown. Join to make fifth row.

6. Join rows to complete center.

7. Appliqué 2 crows as shown in photo. Backstitch legs using three strands of black embroidery floss. Add 1 small button for eye to each crow.

Detail showing crow placement.

Backstitch smoke from chimneys in P and Q blocks.

8. Add black inner side borders to quilt. Add black top and bottom borders.

9. Add green outer side borders to quilt. Add green top and bottom borders.

Quilting and Finishing

1. Layer backing, batting, and quilt top; baste.

2. Quilt as desired. Quilt shown is outline-quilted in Tree block, with stars in F triangles. Houses are quilted in-the-ditch, with Xs in windows. All other blocks are either outline-quilted or quilted in Xs. Outer border has stars.

3. Join 2¼"-wide red strips into 1 continuous piece for straight-grain French-fold binding. Add binding to quilt.

Backstitch Diagram

Designer Gallery

Betsy Shannon
Minneapolis, Minnesota

*I*n the Spring of 1999, wanting to make something to comfort her gravely ill brother, Betsy Shannon made her first simple quilt using fabric that conveyed her brother's artistic interests. She jumped in with both feet, cutting all of her brand new fabric stash into 3" squares! Later she learned many time-saving techniques, but she still sewed all those squares back together, making 24 lap and baby quilts, and learning a lot about color, design, and ¼" seams in the process. Her brother's positive response sparked an artistic outlet for her favorite medium—working with color and texture through fabric and thread.

Betsy hopes to feed the souls of others as well as her own. While she continues to enjoy traditional designs, art quilts that send a message of hope or social justice, or that tell a story, have become her passion.

"Every person on this earth deserves a place to live, food to eat, an education, a loving family, and an accepting community."

Betsy's work has received international attention. She won honorable mention for the 2000 Cocheco Print Works collection, sponsored by the American Textile History Museum. Her quilt remains in their archives. She made *Spirits Rising* in response to the September 11 tragedies. That quilt, in addition to *Wishes for the World,* was in the "America: From the Heart" exhibit in Houston, Texas, that raised $25,615 for the victims' families. The exhibit fostered a book, *America: From the Heart.* Proceeds will benefit the families. Her quilt was chosen for the book's cover.

Wishes for the World
2000, 87" x 88"

Betsy's inspiration for this quilt came from her place of employment, a church in a poor neighborhood of Minneapolis, Minnesota. Their main mission is that of Human Services, serving many ethnic groups and varied religious beliefs. They offer overnight shelter to homeless men, a transitional home for American Indian women, job and housing support to homeless families, and a program of renewal for former offenders. The church also supports a social and spiritual program for mentally challenged adults, a social justice action program, a senior nursing home, and a free store.

The quilt's message, seemingly profound, is simple: "Every person on this earth deserves a place to live, food to eat, an education, a loving family, and an accepting, welcoming community," says Betsy. "As these basic needs are met, all would share in the gift of each other's uniqueness and all would join together in the care and respect of our planet. Then there would be no space or time for hatred. These wishes for the world, I pray."

Wishes for the World was exhibited in the "America: From the Heart" exhibit during the 2001 International Quilt Festival in Houston, Texas. It won 2nd place in the Innovative Category and a Judge's Choice award at the 2001 Minnesota Quilt Festival in Duluth, Minnesota. It was also exhibited in the sanctuary of the Church of St. Stephen in Minneapolis, Minnesota during the 2000 Advent season.

Nancy S. Brown
Oakland, California

Nancy Brown comes from a rich quilting heritage. "My mother took a quilting class about 15 years ago, and I thought it looked interesting," Nancy explains. "So she taught me how to quilt." There were other quilters on both sides of the family, including a great-grandmother and an uncle. "My uncle made quilts for a living after he was disabled in a farming accident," says Nancy. "I wasn't fortunate enough to meet him or my great-grandmother—they died before I was born. But I do have a couple of their beautiful quilts to remember them by."

An active member of the East Bay Heritage Quilters, Nancy considers quilting a wonderful form of artistic expression and an important part of her life. She tries to communicate her personal convictions through her quilts.

"I hope to show [animals'] beauty and their importance in the world and how they deserve to be preserved."

"I have always made appliqué animal quilts, because I love animals and want to celebrate them in my quilts. I hope to show their beauty and their importance in the world and how they deserve to be preserved. My quilts are original designs, and I use mostly appliqué because it allows me to achieve the amount of detail that I want. I like to use a lot of prints, as they add texture. I also like to do extensive quilting to add dimension."

Nancy's quilts are juried into many national shows, and several have been published in quilting magazines.

Mouse Opossum   Tree Frog   Piranha

Amazon Album
1998, 56" x 56"

Nancy Brown loves animals; they are frequently the subject of her fabulous prize-winning quilts.

"I wanted to create an original design in the style of a Baltimore Album and incorporate a lot of wildlife," says Nancy. "I chose animals from the rain forest region near the Amazon River in South America, because there is such a diversity of wildlife and many of the animals are very colorful."

Nancy featured smaller animals in the central blocks, including the blue piranha, the green tree frogs, and the wreath of vine snakes. She made the borders extra wide so she could include medium-sized animals such as the squirrel monkey and the toucan.

"I snuck in one large animal— the anaconda—by only having a small portion of the snake in the upper left corner," says Nancy. "I

then connected the animals in the border with several different vines."

Amazon Album was juried into the 1998 International Quilt Festival in Houston, Texas, and into the 1999 American Quilter's Society show in Paducah, Kentucky. It won Best Interpretation of Theme in the World Quilt Competition in 1999 and also won Best of Show in the 1999 Quilts at the Crossroads in Flint, Michigan.

Cassandra Williams
Grants Pass, Oregon

Cassandra Williams has been quilting off and on for about 40 years. "Oil painting was always my passion," Cassandra says. "Upon retirement six years ago, I moved to Oregon. The drastic change from the Las Vegas desert inspired me. I put away my paints and gathered fabrics instead! Art quilts have been my passion now for three years."

Cassandra is active in several local quilt guilds, including the Hugo Schoolhouse Quilters, Piecemakers, and the Mountain Stars Guild. She is also a member of several national quilting organizations.

"I love the creativity of an art quilt."

"A quilter is who I am," she declares. "I love the creativity of an art quilt. Each piece leads me into ideas for several more."

Encounter Trio

Encounter Trio
2000, 32" x 43"

"This trio of quilts is a rendering of the earth, air, and water theme," Cassandra explains. "I try to install an element of danger in my nature quilts," Cassandra continues. "Here, the geese search for safe harbor, while the sharp-eyed blue heron guards his territory. The fish and turtle are startled to be sharing a stream—each uncertain if this encounter will make him prey or predator!"

Encounter Trio is actually three separate quilts that were then stitched together to form one art piece. It has been exhibited in Oregon at the Hugo Schoolhouse Show, the Mountain Stars Guild Show, and the Jacksonville Museum Show, all in 2001. It was also a finalist at the International Quilt Festival in Houston, Texas, in October 2001. In May 2002, it won third place in machine quilting at the Northwest Quilters Show in Portland, Oregon.

Here, Kitty, Kitty
2001, 37" x 41"

Cassandra lives in a mountainous area of Oregon where she see cougars on occasion. "The probability of imminent danger is well expressed by this cougar," she says. "He appears intent, but at rest. But wait! Look carefully and realize his scrutiny of you, his bunched muscles in the ready for a swift attack. Don't call, 'Here, kitty, kitty!'"

This quilt was exhibited at the Mountain Stars Guild Show in Medford, Oregon, in April 2001. In July, it won first place in wall hangings at the Jacksonville Museum Show in Jacksonville, Oregon. By October, it was a finalist at the International Quilt Festival in Houston, Texas. In April 2002, it won first place and best of show at the Umpqua Valley Quilt Show in Roseburg, Oregon. In May 2002, it won second place in machine quilting and third place in innovation at the Northwest Quilters Show in Portland, Oregon.

Patricia M. Goffette
Edmonds, Washington

*P*atricia M. Goffette is an active member of three quilting guilds: Quilters Anonymous, the Association of Pacific Northwest Quilters, Contemporary Concepts, and the International Quilt Association. When she started quilting in the early 1990s, Patricia didn't know she could purchase traditional quilting patterns—so she made her own.

"I began using fabrics in a new way, much like brush strokes," says Patricia. "I started using squares and triangles, but now I use completely freeform shapes and lots of basting to form the images." Patricia uses natural fabrics from all over the world. She hand appliqués them in place and then machine quilts them to suggest natural vegetation or hair on an animal.

Fabric selection is key to Patricia's look. "The backing fabric for Bamboo Bear was manufactured and purchased in the same province in China in which the panda bears live," she explains. "Fabrics fascinate me. Everything about them is fun—the colors, the patterns, the textures. It is intriguing what can be done with textiles."

"Fabrics fascinate me. Everything about them is fun—the colors, the patterns, the textures."

In between her "critter quilts," Patricia manages to make a few quilts each year for her family and friends and their children. "Quite often I have several quilts going on at one time," she confesses. "Sometimes I must step back from a particularly perplexing project and distance myself from the quilt. When I come back, I'll look at it with a fresh eye and the solution comes to me. I may find that the best piece of fabric was right before me the whole time. Or I'll shuffle through my stash and a piece of fabric seems to jump out, as if saying, 'Try me!'"

Bamboo Bear
2000, 38" x 58"

Bamboo Bear is one in a series of quilts that Patricia M. Goffette is creating on endangered species. Speaking of the panda in this quilt, Patricia says, "He usually wanders alone looking for his favorite morsels to eat. It seems that as each year goes by, there are fewer and fewer mates in the forest."

This stunning masterpiece won a second place ribbon at the Quilters Anonymous Quilt Show in Monroe, Washington, in 2000.

Later that year, it won Best Innovative Quilt at the Great Pacific Northwest Quiltfest in Seattle, Washington. It was also juried into the International Quilt Festival at Houston, Texas, in 2001.

Tonya Littmann
Denton, Texas

Tonya Littmann grew up admiring quilts made by her grandmother and great-grandmother, but didn't start quilting until 1989 at age 29. She made her first quilt from hand-dyed and batik fabrics she made at a fiber arts retreat. Possessing only basic sewing skills, she quickly realized that she needed some help.

"I enrolled in a beginning quilting continuing education class at the University of North Texas and made a traditional sampler quilt in Amish colors," says Tonya. "I've made many traditional pieced quilts since then, but I always had to change something to make it my own."

Before coming to quiltmaking, Tonya painted in watercolors and acrylics in a photo-realistic style. She couldn't figure out how to translate her style into fabric until she was introduced to the "snippet" style of quiltmaking in 1999. She attended a lecture and workshop by Cindy Walter, author of *Snippet Sensations,* and found her niche. "Even though I feel the need to make a garment or a pieced quilt now and then, I have found a comfortable style that combines my photo-realistic tendencies with my need to create in fabric," says Tonya.

"I have found a comfortable style that combines my photo-realistic tendencies with my need to create in fabric."

Tonya is a professional graphic designer who owns her own business. She is also a wife and mother. "My husband Jon rides his Harley Davidson whenever he can get time away from his dental laboratory," says Tonya. "In order to include both me *and* our son Berek on his rides, I learned to ride and bought my own Harley in 2000. The motorcycles turn an outing into an event and give my husband a hobby when I go on a quilt or fiber-art retreat."

"My business requires me to satisfy the design needs and tastes of my clients in their time frames," Tonya says. "Quilting is an escape for me to create with no input from anyone else unless I ask for it. It also connects me to my past, as I continue to create in the medium of my grandmothers."

Kat's Cats
2001, 29¼" x 24¼"

Each year, the Show Chair of the Dallas Quilt Celebration selects a theme for the quilt show and the Show Chair's Category. "The theme for the 2001 show was 'cats,' and I wanted to create another snippet art quilt," says Tonya. "I mentioned to my friend Kathi Casey that I was looking for inspiration for the cat theme. She reminded me of a photograph I'd taken of her cat family huddled together during a rainstorm."

Tonya completed the quilt in three months, after painstakingly placing fused slivers of fabric onto muslin with tweezers. She machine-quilted the piece in 23 hours during the Denton Quilt Guild Spring Retreat in 2001.

Kat's Cats won first place in the Show Chair's Category at the 2001 Dallas Quilt Celebration. It was also juried into the Pictoral Quilts category at the 2001 International Quilt Festival.

Irene Brown Barker
Warren, Maine

*I*rene Brown Barker has been quilting for more than 30 years. It began when she saw a quilt in a decorating magazine and decided that she needed it for her guest room. "I ordered the pattern," she recalls. "I knew nothing about what I was trying to do. There were no quilt shops, so the local fabric shop had to suffice. I still have that quilt, and I use it often."

While Irene spends most of her time in Maine, her husband's job takes them to Jasper, Georgia, in the winter. This allows her to be part of the East Cobb Quilt Guild in the Atlanta, Georgia, area, as well as her own Pine Tree Quilters Guild, Inc., in Warren, Maine.

> *"I like to send the children in my life out into the world with a quilt for comfort, should they ever need it."*

"Quilting has become my art form, and it appeals to my New England practicality," Irene says. "I can construct something pleasing to my eye that also has a useful purpose. My quilts usually have a traditional look to them. If the pattern is not traditional, then I still use reproduction prints to make it. I love all the reproduction fabric that is currently available."

If she's not making quilts, Irene is definitely thinking about them. "I usually have at least two quilts in my head, as well as others in various stages of design and construction," she says. "I also use old fabrics and squares whenever I can. I like to send the children in my life out into the world with a quilt for comfort, should they ever need it."

Star Flower

Noonday

Whirlwind

Fantastic 4th
2000, 88" x 94"

Fantastic 4th combines a variety of challenging quilt techniques. It won the Oxmoor House Sponsorship Award at Georgia Celebrates Quilts at the East Cobb Quilt Guild Show in Marietta, Georgia, in 2001.

"This quilt is my interpretation of a 19th-century quilt I saw in an old calendar," says Irene. "I thought it was wonderfully appeal-ing, and both my son and grand-son have a penchant for flag quilts. The challenge for me was trying to figure out how the original might have been contructed and to make my quilt look like it was from the 19th century."

There are many traditional elements within this quilt. LeMoyne Stars make up the flag's field of stars, and the flag itself is surround-ed by a pyramid border. The blocks surrounding the flag are known as A Striking Pattern or Noonday. Followed by a diamond border are Whirlwind blocks (the ones that look like peppermint candy) and a block called both Star Flower and Golden Glow. Although the color scheme may seem unconventional for a patriotic quilt, it is historically accurate for the period.

Ricky Tims
Arvada, Colorado

A native of Wichita Falls, Texas, Ricky Tims recently moved to Arvada, Colorado—a suburb of Denver. He still considers himself a Texan. Even his business card reads, "Ricky Tims: Texan, Musician, Quilter."

And it's not unusual for Ricky to identify his passions in that order. Quilting is a relatively new interest for him, compared to his lifelong love for music. He began formal music lessons at the age of three. He is a conductor, composer, arranger, music producer, and performing artist. He has recorded several CDs of his original music. He also implemented and conducted the 1998 concert "When We No Longer Touch," featuring the St. Louis Voices United Chorus and members of the St. Louis Symphony Orchestra.

Now a professional quilter, Ricky teaches an exciting variety of workshops that encourage people to cultivate self-expression. He maintains an extensive international schedule of engagements. One of his most popular presentations is a combination of his life story, slides of his quilts, and live music that he performs. In it, he tells the humorous story of how he came into quilting after his grandmother gave him her 1956 Kenmore sewing machine in 1991. (We won't spoil the story by telling you about his grandmother!)

"...things don't always turn out the way you expect them to."

For more about Ricky and his work, visit his Web site at: www.rickytims.com

Songe d'Automne
2000, 86" x 86"

Ricky Tims used his own original multi-colored hand-dyed cotton fabrics to make this quilt. It is completely machine pieced, machine appliquéd, and machine quilted. Trapunto (stuffing to create dimension) lies under each appliqué, with additional trapunto in the quilting. The title, *Songe d'Automne,* comes from a popular waltz played by the ship's orchestra as the Titanic was sinking.

Songe d'Automne won Best of Show at the Mid-Atlantic Quilt Festival in February 2000. It later won the $5000 Pfaff Master Award for Machine Artistry at the International Quilt Festival in Houston, Texas, in October 2000.

Ricky's goal in planning this quilt was to make a traditional quilt design with a contemporary feel, allowing color to flow on color.

"I drew the original design with straight lines, and I intended to use fabrics in traditional Amish colors," says Ricky. "That's proof that things don't always turn out the way you expect them to."

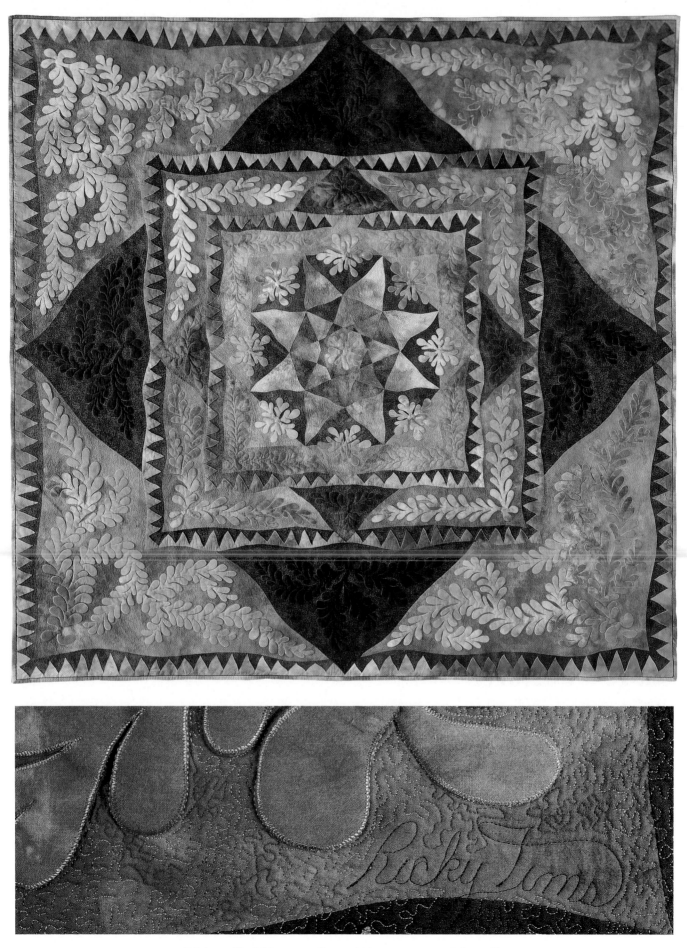

Ricky quilted his name discreetly in one corner of the quilt.

Amy Stewart Winsor
Cary, North Carolina

A native of Oklahoma, Amy Winsor met her husband in college at Brigham Young, where she earned a bachelor's degree in Clothing and Textiles. After living in Utah for 10 years, they moved to North Carolina in 1987. That was about the time her interest in quilting took off. By 1993, she was teaching quilt classes and began curating the Page-Walker Art Quilt Shows in Cary, North Carolina. Her quilts have won many national awards and have been featured in galleries and on television.

As the mother of six children, Amy has always believed it was important to make time for her own happiness. She began to realize that if she was doing a technique that wasn't fun, her quilting time was failing to give her the escape she was seeking. She quickly realized that she has the most fun when she makes quilts that use no math or require no precision piecing.

"Playing with fabric, old jewelry, buttons, beads, and recycled treasures brings out my creativity and makes me happy."

"I call myself mathophobic," says Amy. "I thrive on designing by eye, not by planning things out beforehand. If it is in my head, it can come out on the fabric. I enjoy telling a story using whimsical appliquéd figures and three-dimensional embellishment. Playing with fabric, old jewelry, buttons, beads, and recycled treasures brings out my creativity and makes me happy. Plus, it gives me an excuse to keep shopping those yard sales!"

Make an Appointment
2001, 66" x 80½"

"I am constantly frustrated at the demands our society places upon me to keep my house presentable," says Amy. "I am mystified by the ideals portrayed in magazines and television, and I wonder if any real person ever keeps a house looking so neat."

The center panel of her quilt says, "If you want to see me, come over anytime. If you want to see my house, MAKE AN APPOINTMENT!" Amy says this accurately states her attitude about her house. With six children, her husband has often referred to her jokingly as the Old Woman in the Shoe, who had so many children, she didn't know what to do.

"The first border includes many of the phrases with which we, as women, have been indoctrinated," says Amy. "Most of these, for me, are hopelessly unreachable. I have filled the outer border with my many reasons for failing to maintain a beautiful, showcase home. All the little day-to-day requirements that fill up my time frustrate my lofty goals.

"The quilt's theme is that no matter how embarrassed I am about the state of my house, life goes on. The sun still shines, the flowers (and dandelions) still bloom, and I can still accept myself and be happy as I deal with everyday emergencies, annoyances, and household maintenance which could drive me crazy."

Make an Appointment *won second place and Judge's Recognition at the National Quilter's Association (NQA) in 2001. It was exhibited in "Art Quilts: Narrative Form" exhibit at the International Quilt Festival in 2001 and the Page-Walker exhibit. It also appeared in the* NQA Quilting Quarterly *magazine in December 2001 and the 2003 AQS Quilt Art Engagement Calendar.*

Quilt Smart Workshop

A Guide to Quiltmaking

❖

Preparing Fabric

Before cutting any pieces, be sure to wash and dry your fabric to preshrink it. All-cotton fabrics may need pressing before cutting. Trim selvages from the fabric before you cut pieces.

Making Templates

Before you can make one of the quilts in this book, you must make templates from the printed patterns given. (Not all pieces require patterns—some pieces are meant to be cut with a rotary cutter and ruler.) Quilters have used many materials to make templates, including cardboard and sandpaper. Transparent template plastic, available at craft supply and quilt shops, is durable, see-through, and easy to use.

To make a plastic template, place the plastic sheet on the printed page and use a laundry marker or permanent fine-tip marking pen to trace each pattern. For machine piecing, trace on the outside solid (cutting) line. For hand piecing, trace on the inside broken (stitching) line. Cut out the template on the traced line. Label each template with the pattern name, letter, grain line arrow, and match points (corner dots).

Marking and Cutting Fabric for Piecing

Place the template facedown on the wrong side of the fabric and mark around it with a sharp pencil.

If you will be piecing by machine, the pencil lines represent cutting lines. Cut on each marked line.

For hand piecing, the pencil lines are seam lines. Leave at least ¾" between marked lines for seam allowances. Add ¼" seam allowance around each piece as you cut. Mark match points (corner dots) on each piece.

You can do without templates if you use a rotary cutter and ruler to cut straight strips and geometric shapes such as squares and triangles. Rotary cutting

is always paired with machine piecing, and pieces are cut with seam allowances included.

Hand Piecing

To hand piece, place two fabric pieces together with right sides facing. Insert a pin in each match point of the top piece. Stick the pin through both pieces and check to be sure that it pierces the match point on the bottom piece (*Figure 1*). Adjust the pieces as necessary to align the match points. (The raw edges of the two pieces may not align exactly.) Pin the pieces securely together.

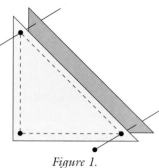

Figure 1.
Aligning Match Points

Sew with a running stitch of 8 to 10 stitches per inch. Sew from match point to match point, checking the stitching as you go to be sure you are sewing in the seam line of both pieces.

To make sharp corners, begin and end the stitching exactly at the match point; do not stitch into the seam allowances. When joining units where several seams come together, do not sew over seam allowances; sew through them at the point where all seam lines meet (*Figure 2*).

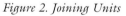
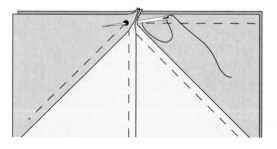

Figure 2. Joining Units

Always press both seam allowances to one side. Pressing the seam open, as in dressmaking, can leave gaps between stitches through which the batting may beard. Press seam allowances toward the darker fabric

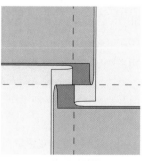

Figure 3.
Pressing Intersecting Seams

whenever you can, but it is sometimes more important to reduce bulk by avoiding overlapping seam allowances. When four or more seams meet at one point, such as at the corner of a block, press all the seams in a "swirl" in the same direction to reduce bulk (*Figure 3*).

Machine Piecing

To machine piece, place two fabric pieces together with right sides facing. Align match points as described under "Hand Piecing" and pin the pieces together securely.

Set the stitch length at 12 to 15 stitches per inch. At this setting, you do not need to backstitch to lock seam beginnings and ends. Use a presser foot that gives a perfect ¼" seam allowance, or measure ¼" from the needle and mark that point on the presser foot with nail polish or masking tape.

Chain piecing, stitching edge to edge, saves time when sewing similar sets of pieces (*Figure 4*). Join the

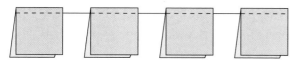

Figure 4. Chain Piecing

first two pieces as usual. At the end of the seam, do not backstitch, cut the thread, or lift the presser foot. Instead, sew a few stitches off the fabric. Place the next two pieces and continue stitching. Keep sewing until all the sets are joined. Then cut the sets apart.

Press seam allowances toward the darker fabric whenever possible. When you join blocks or rows, press the seam allowances of the top row in one direction and the seam allowances of the bottom row in the opposite direction to help ensure that the seams will lie flat (*Figure 5*).

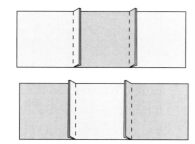

Figure 5. Pressing Seams for Machine Piecing

Hand Appliqué

Hand appliqué is the best way to achieve the look of traditional appliqué. But using freezer paper, which

is sold in grocery stores, saves time because it eliminates the need for hand basting seam allowances.

Make templates without seam allowances. Trace the template onto the *dull* side of the freezer paper; cut the paper on the marked line. Make a freezer-paper shape for each piece to be appliquéd.

Pin the freezer-paper shape, *shiny side up*, to the *wrong side* of the fabric. Following the paper shape and adding a scant ¼" seam allowance, cut out the fabric piece. Do not remove the pins. Use the tip of a hot, dry iron to press the seam allowance to the shiny side of the freezer paper. Be careful not to touch the shiny side of the freezer paper with the iron. Remove the pins.

Pin the appliqué shape in place on the background fabric. Use one strand of sewing thread in a color to match the appliqué shape. Using a very small slipstitch (*Figure 6*) or blindstitch (*Figure 7*), appliqué the shape to the background fabric.

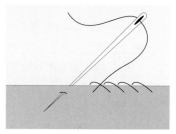

Figure 6. Slipstitch

When your stitching is complete, cut away the background fabric behind the appliqué, leaving ¼" seam allowance. Separate the freezer paper from the fabric with your fingernail and pull gently to remove it.

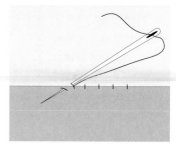

Figure 7. Blindstitch

Mitering Borders

Mitered borders take a little extra care to stitch but offer a nice finish when square border corners just won't do.

First, measure the length of the quilt through the middle of the quilt top. Cut two border strips to fit this length, plus the width of the border plus 2". Centering the measurement on the strip, place pins on the edge of each strip at the center and each end of the measurement. Match the pins on each border strip to the corners of a long side of the quilt. Starting and stopping ¼" from each corner of the quilt, sew the borders to the quilt, easing the quilt to fit between the pins (*Figure 8*). Press seam allowances toward border strip.

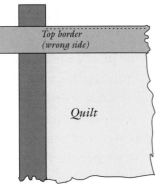

Figure 8

Measure the quilt width through the middle and cut two border strips to fit, adding the border width plus 2". Join these borders to opposite ends of the quilt in the same manner.

Fold one border corner over the adjacent corner (*Figure 9*) and press. On the wrong side, stitch in the creased fold to stitch a mitered seam (*Figure 10*). Press; then check to make sure the corner lies flat on the quilt top. Trim seam allowances.

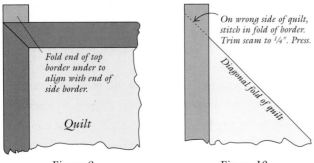

Figure 9

Figure 10

Marking Your Quilt Top

When the quilt top is complete, press it thoroughly before marking it with quilting designs. The most popular methods for marking use stencils or templates. Both can be purchased, or you can make your own. You can also use a yardstick to mark straight lines or grids.

Use a silver quilter's pencil for marking light to medium fabrics and a white chalk pencil on dark fabrics. Lightly mark the quilt top with your chosen quilting designs.

Making a Backing

The instructions in *Great American Quilts* give backing yardage based on 45"-wide fabric unless a 90"-wide or 108"-wide backing is more practical. (These fabrics are sold at fabric and quilt shops.) Pieced or not, the quilt backing should be at least 3" larger on all sides than the quilt top.

Backing fabric should be of a type and color that is compatible with the quilt top. Percale sheets are not recommended, because they are tightly woven and difficult to hand-quilt through.

A pieced backing for a bed quilt should have three panels. The three-panel backing is recommended because it tends to wear better and lie flatter than the two-panel type, the center seam of which often makes a ridge down the center of the quilt. Begin by cutting the fabric in half widthwise (*Figure 11*).

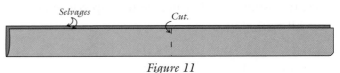

Figure 11

Open the two lengths and stack them, with right sides facing and selvages aligned. Stitch along both selvage edges to create a tube of fabric (*Figure 12*). Cut down the center of the top layer of fabric *only* and open the fabric flat (*Figure 13*). Press seam allowances toward center panel.

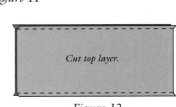

Figure 12

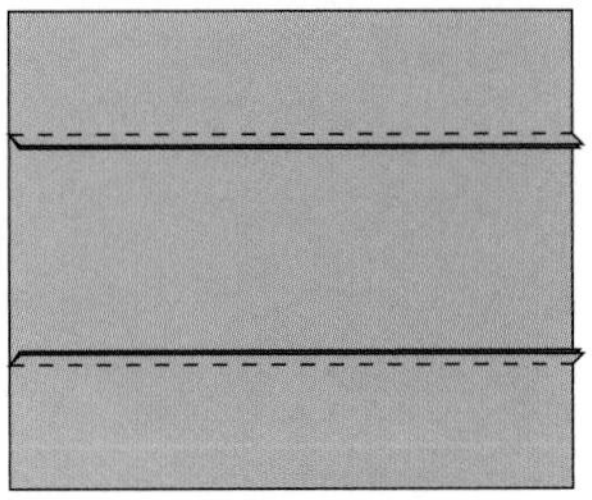

Figure 13

Layering and Basting

Prepare a working surface to spread out the quilt. Place the backing on the surface, right side down. Unfold the batting and place it on top of the backing. Smooth any wrinkles or lumps in the batting. Lay the quilt top right side up on top of the batting and backing. Make sure backing and quilt top are parallel.

Use a darning needle for basting, with a long strand of sewing thread. Begin in the center of your quilt and baste out toward the edges. The stitches should cover enough of the quilt to keep the layers from shifting during quilting. Inadequate basting can result in puckers and folds on the back and front of the quilt during quilting.

Hand Quilting

Hand quilting can be done with the quilt in a hoop or in a floor frame. It is best to start in the middle of your quilt and quilt out toward the edges.

Most quilters use a thin, short needle called a "between." Betweens are available in sizes 7 to 12, with 7 being the longest and 12 the shortest. If you are a beginning quilter, try a size 7 or 8. Because betweens are so much shorter than other needles, they may feel awkward at first. As your skill increases, try using a smaller needle to help you make smaller stitches.

Quilting thread, heavier and stronger than sewing thread, is available in a wide variety of colors. If color matching is critical and you can't find the color you need, you can substitute cotton sewing thread if you coat it with beeswax before quilting to prevent it from tangling.

Thread your needle with a 20" length and make a small knot at one end. Insert the needle into the quilt top approximately ½" from the point where you want to begin quilting. Do not take the needle through all three layers, but stop it in the batting and bring it up through the quilt top again at your starting point. Tug gently on the thread to pop the knot through the quilt top into the batting. This anchors the thread without an unsightly knot showing on the back.

With your non-sewing hand underneath the quilt, insert the needle with the point straight down in the quilt about ¹⁄₁₆" from the starting point. With your underneath finger, feel for the point as the needle comes through the backing (*Figure 14*).

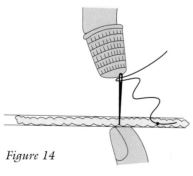

Figure 14

Place the thumb of your sewing hand approximately ½" ahead of the needle. When you feel the needle touch your underneath finger, push the fabric up from below as you rock the needle down to a nearly horizontal position. Using the thumb of your sewing hand in conjunction with the underneath hand, pinch a little hill

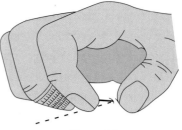

Figure 15

in the fabric and push the tip of the needle back through the quilt top (*Figure 15*).

Now either push the needle all the way through to complete one stitch or rock the needle again to an upright position on its point to take another stitch. Take no more than a quarter-needleful of stitches before pulling the needle through.

When you have 6" of thread remaining, you must end the old thread securely and invisibly. Carefully tie a knot in the thread, flat against the surface of the fabric. Pop the knot through the top as you did when beginning the line of quilting. Clip the thread, rethread your needle, and continue quilting.

Machine Quilting

Machine quilting is as old as the sewing machine itself; but until recently, it was thought inferior to hand quilting. Fine machine quilting is an exclusive category, but it requires a different set of skills from hand quilting.

Machine quilting can be done on your sewing machine using a straight stitch and a special presser foot. A walking foot or even-feed foot is recommended for straight-line quilting to help the top fabric move through the machine at the same rate that the feed dogs move the bottom fabric.

Regular sewing thread or nylon thread can be used for machine quilting. With the quilt top facing you, roll the long edges of the basted quilt toward the center, leaving a 12"-wide area unrolled in the center. Secure the roll with bicycle clips, metal bands that are available at quilt shops. Begin at one unrolled end and fold the quilt over and over until only a small area is showing. This will be the area where you will begin to quilt.

Place the folded portion of the quilt in your lap. Start quilting in the center and work to the right, unfolding and unrolling the quilt as you go. Remove the quilt from the machine, turn it, and reinsert it in the machine to stitch the left side. A table placed behind your sewing machine will help support the quilt as it is stitched.

Curves and circles are most easily made by free-motion machine quilting. Using a darning foot and with the feed dogs down, move the quilt under the needle with your fingertips. Place your hands on the fabric on each side of the foot and run the machine at a steady, medium speed. The length of the stitches is determined by the rate of speed at which you move fabric through the machine. Do not rotate the quilt; rather, move it from side to side as needed. Always stop with the needle down to keep the quilt from shifting.

Making Binding

A continuous bias or straight-grain strip is used to bind quilt edges. Bias binding is especially recommended for quilts with curved edges. Follow these steps to make a continuous bias strip:

1. Start with a square of fabric. Multiply the number of binding inches needed by the cut width of the binding strip (usually 2½"). Use a calculator to find the square root of that number. That's the size of the fabric square needed to make your binding.

2. Cut the square in half diagonally.

3. With right sides facing, join triangles to form a sawtooth as shown *(Figure 16)*.

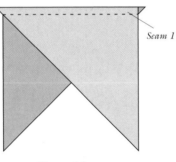

Figure 16

4. Press seam open.

Mark off parallel lines the desired width of the binding as shown *(Figure 17)*.

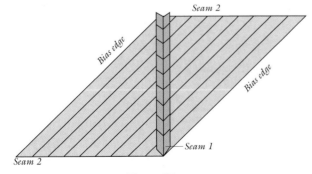

Figure 17

5. With right sides facing, align raw edges marked Seam 2. Offset edges by one strip width, so one side is higher than the other *(Figure 18)*. Stitch Seam 2. Press seam open.

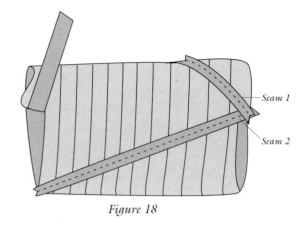

Figure 18

6. Cut the binding in a continuous strip, starting with the protruding point and following the marked lines around the tube.

7. Press the binding strip in half lengthwise, with wrong sides facing.

Attaching Binding

To prepare your quilt for binding, baste the layers together ¼" from the edge of the quilt. Trim the backing and batting even with the edge of the quilt top. Beginning at the midpoint of one side of the quilt, pin the binding to the top, with right sides facing and raw edges aligned.

Machine-stitch the binding along one edge of the quilt, sewing through all layers. Backstitch at the beginning of the seam to lock the stitching.

Stitch until you reach the seam line at the corner, and backstitch. Lift the presser foot and turn the quilt to align the foot with the next edge. Miter fabric at corner. Continue sewing around all four sides. Join the beginning and end of the binding strip by machine.

Turn the binding over the edge and blindstitch it in place on the backing. At each corner, fold the excess binding neatly to make a mitered corner and blindstitch it in place.